# ELEMENTARY
## MY DEAR WATSON

# ELEMENTARY
## MY DEAR WATSON

### SHERLOCK HOLMES
### CENTENARY

#### HIS LIFE & TIMES

Graham Nown

Salem House Publishers
Topsfield, Massachusetts

# Acknowledgments

The author wishes to thank Canongate Publishing for permission to quote from *The Casebook of a Victorian Detective*, and A.P. Watt for permission to use an extract from Hesketh Pearson's biography of Conan Doyle.

All the colour photographs in this book were taken by Helen Pask except for the following:

Mary Evans Picture Library, London, facing pages 33 and 128

Fine Art Photographs, London, facing pages 65 and 129

The publishers would like to thank the following for allowing material from their collections to be photographed:

City of Westminster Libraries: Sherlock Holmes Collection, Marylebone Library, facing pages 17 and 64

Catherine Cooke, facing pages 112 and 113

The Stanley MacKenzie Collection, facing pages 16, 32, 80 and 81

The illustration of William Gillette on page 41 is reproduced courtesy of the Mander and Mitchenson Theatre Collection.

First published in the United States by
Salem House Publishers, 1987
462 Boston Street, Topsfield, MA 01983

Cover Illustration by Robin Lawrie

Printed and bound in Spain

LIBRARY OF CONGRESS CATALOG NUMBER:
86–62242

ISBN: 0 88162 2613

# Contents

FOR SYLVANA
Who did the detective work

'You will remember, Watson, how the dreadful business of the Abernetty family was first brought to my notice by the depth which the parsley had sunk into the butter upon a hot day ...'

*Sherlock Holmes*

# A Study in Scarlet

Holmes and Watson as they appeared in the 1893 Ward Lock edition of *A Study in Scarlet*.

# From the Introduction to the Ward Lock Edition of 1893

## Publisher's Note

As it is in *A Study In Scarlet* that Mr Sherlock Holmes is first introduced to the public, and his methods of work described, it occurred to the publishers of the volume that a paper on 'Sherlock Holmes', which Dr Doyle's old master, Dr Joseph Bell, the original of Sherlock Holmes, contributed recently to *The Bookman,* would greatly interest readers who did not see it when it appeared in that publication.

Dr Bell's 'intuitive powers' in dealing with his patients were, so his pupil, Dr Doyle, tells us in the pages of *The Strand Magazine,* 'simply marvellous.'

As Mr Sherlock Holmes has now become a household word and almost a public institution, the publishers of 'A Study In Scarlet' hope that the following paper, in which particulars of Dr Doyle's early education and training, and of the circumstances which led him to form the habit of making careful observations, will prove of interest to his many readers.

# 'Mr Sherlock Holmes' by Dr Joseph Bell

DR CONAN DOYLE has made a well-deserved success for his detective stories, and made the name of his hero beloved by the boys of this country by the marvellous cleverness of his method. He shows how easy it is, if only you can observe, to find out a great deal as to the works and ways of your innocent and unconscious friends, and, by an extension of the same method, to baffle the criminal and lay bare the manner of his crime.

Dr Conan Doyle's education as a student of medicine taught him how to observe, and his practice, both as a general practitioner and a specialist, has been splendid training for a man such as he is, gifted with eyes, memory and imagination. Eyes and ears which can see and hear, memory to record at once and to recall at pleasure the impressions of the senses, and an imagination capable of weaving a theory or piecing together a broken chain or unravelling a tangled clue, such are implements of his trade to a successful diagnostician. If in addition the doctor is also a born story-teller, then it is a mere matter of choice whether he writes detective stories or keeps his strength for a great historical romance as is *The White Company*. Syme, one of the greatest teachers of surgical diagnosis that ever lived, had a favourite illustration which, as a tradition of his school, has made a mark on Dr Conan Doyle's method: 'Try to learn the features of a disease or injury as precisely as you know the features, the gait, the tricks of manner of your most intimate friend.' Him, even in a crowd, you can recognise at once; it may be a crowd of men dressed alike, and each having his complement of eyes, nose, hair and limbs; in every essential they resemble each other, only in trifles do they differ; and yet, by knowing these trifles well, you make your diagnosis or recognition with ease.

Trained as he has been to notice and appreciate minute detail, Dr Doyle saw how he could interest his intelligent readers by taking them into his confidence, and showing his mode of working. He created a shrewd, quick-sighted, inquisitive man, half doctor, half virtuoso, with plenty of spare time, a retentive memory, and perhaps with the best gift of all – the power of unloading the mind of all the burden of trying to remember unnecessary details. Holmes tells Watson: 'A man should keep his little brain-attic stocked with all the furniture that he is likely to use, as the rest he can put away in the lumber-room of his library, where he can get it if he wants it.' But to him the petty results of environment, the sign-manuals of labour, the stains of trade, the incidents of travel, have living interest, as they tend to satisfy the insatiable, almost inhuman, because impersonal curiosity. He puts the man in the position of an amateur, and therefore irresponsible, detective, who is consulted in all sorts of cases, and then lets us see how he works. He makes him explain to the good Watson the trivial, or apparently trivial, links in his chain of evidence. These are at once so obvious, when explained, and so easy once you know them, that the ingenuous reader at once feels and says to himself, I could also do this; life is not so dull after all; I will keep my eyes open, and find out things. The gold watch, with its scratched keyhole and pawn-broker's marks, told such an easy tale about Watson's brother. The dusty old billy-cock hat revealed that its master had taken to drinking some years ago, and had got his hair cut yesterday. The tiny thorn-prick and fearsome footmark of the thing that was neither a child nor a monkey enabled Holmes to identify and capture the Anda-man Islander. Yet, after all, you say, there is nothing wonderful; we could all do the same.

The experienced physician and the trained surgeon every day, in their examinations of the humblest patient, have to go through a similar process of reasoning, quick or slow according to the personal equations of each, almost automatic in the experienced man, laboured and often er-ratic in the tyro, yet requiring just the same simple requisites, senses to notice facts, and education and intelligence to apply them. Mere acuteness of the senses is not enough. Your Indian tracker will tell you that the footprint on the leaves was not a redskin's, but a paleface's, because it marked a shoe-print, but it needs an expert in shoe-leather to tell where that shoe was made. A sharp-eyed detective may notice the thumb-mark of a grimy or bloody hand on the velvet or the mirror, but it needs all the scientific knowledge of a Galton to render the ridges and furrows of the stain visible and perma-nent, and then to identify by their sign-manual the suspected thief or murderer. Sherlock Holmes had acute senses, and the special education and information that make these valuable; and he can afford to let us into the secrets of his method. But in addition to the creation of his hero, Dr Conan Doyle in this remarkable series of stories has proved himself a born story-teller. He has had the wit to devise excellent plots, interesting complications; he tells them in honest Saxon-English with direct-ness and pith; and, above all his other merits, his stories are absolutely free from padding. He knows how delicious brevity is, how everything tends to be too long, and he has given us stories that we can read at a sitting between dinner and coffee, and we have not a chance to forget the beginning before we reach the end. The ordinary detective story, from Gaboriau or Boisgobey down to the latest shocker, really needs an effort of memory quite misplaced to keep the circumstances of the crimes and all the wrong scents of the various meddlers before the wearied reader. Dr Doyle never gives you a chance to forget an incident or miss a point.

# PART I

# The Adventure of the Disillusioned Doctor

Conan Doyle.

# Conan Doyle, Holmes and Strand Magazine

HOLMES HIMSELF would not have been out of place among the intellectual, slightly Bohemian gathering of two hundred distinguished mourners assembled on the sweeping summer lawn of a picturesque Crowborough house in 1930. Newspapers, with the weighty patriotism summoned for such occasions, recorded the sad passing of Sir Arthur Conan Doyle before plunging into other matters of concern, such as the crash of the Bombay cotton market and a disturbing fall in Brazilian securities. In Sussex the mood was one of hope. A gentle breeze rustled the evergreen shrubbery and ruffled a line of tall pines towering above a simple wooden summer house in the corner of the garden. Inside, on a rustic table, lay a pile of blank writing-paper, an inkpot and a pen.

The mourners, many of them spiritualists, sang 'Open My Eyes That I May See' as Paddy, his Airedale terrier, rolled on the grass. The coffin, laden with red roses, was carried from the ivy-smothered house past Lady Doyle in her grey dress and the pale prints of the other guests; there was a noticeable absence of black. Sir Arthur was buried a few feet away from the summer house, as though he might, if inspiration took him, pick up his writing tools again. 'There is no death – only eternal life', Lady 'Billy' Doyle bravely intoned. 'The message rang out with conviction', reported the *Daily Telegraph*, 're-echoing through the encircling trees, it was easy to believe that the spirit which had shaken off its physical garment was very near his beloved ones.'

Lady Doyle read her tribute in a clear voice which carried through the heat haze to an open window of the house where one of their sons lay in bed with laryngitis. She recalled her husband's 'unselfish life, his courage, his fearlessness, his championship of those suffering injustice, his help to those in need and sorrow . . .' And had Holmes – literature's most lifelike figure – been there, those weary, heavy-lidded eyes might have moistened, as though he were listening to a eulogy on his great companion, Dr Watson.

Doyle shared few of Holmes's attributes, except perhaps for a terrier-like persistence in seeing justice done. Physically he resembled the image which in the past hundred years we have come to associate with Watson. The master detective was gaunt and angular, an intellectual machine fired by restless energy, skilled at masking his inadequacies and prone to moods of deep reflection. Doyle was bluff and thick-set with a squat nose, remodelled from years of boxing, and an Irish buoyancy which gave him a natural ability to get along with everyone he met. Although the amiable GP personally solved two notable miscarriages of justice, his powers of observation were not always equal to the character he created.

Doyle's biographer, Hesketh Pearson, recalled being told by a senior ophthalmic surgeon that Doyle took his daughter to have her eyes examined in 1918: 'I remember being shaken to the core that Sherlock Holmes had only just found out, what must have been evident to the most casual observer for months, if not years, that the child was as blind as a bat for objects only a few yards from her face, because of her uncorrected myopia.'

The Holmes stories, too, are peppered with mistakes, contradictions and inconsistencies but, as Pearson argues, so too was Shakespeare – and no-one gives a rap when a character gives so much delight. Holmes, in many ways, was all the things Doyle was not, but his creation was by no means a compensation. Of the two, the author was the more sociable; a likeable, avuncular bear of a man with virtues instantly recognizable to those he met.

Holmes was born from Dr Doyle's failure to build a thriving medical practice. He had suffered poverty for most of his life and turned to writing for both release and reward. The partnership began at the sitting-room table of a modest villa in Southsea, and blossomed at 2 Devonshire Place, a consulting-room near enough to Wimpole Street to attract potential patients, but too far away for any of them to consider the practice fashionable. 'There', said Conan Doyle, 'for £120 a year I got the use of a front room with part use of a waiting-room. I was soon to find that they were both waiting-rooms. Every morning I walked from my lodgings at Montagu Place, reached my consulting-room at ten, and sat there until three or four, with never a ring to disturb my security... It was ideal, and so long as I was thoroughly unsuccessful in my professional venture there was every chance of improvement in my literary prospects.'

Doyle's early writing efforts had met with mixed success. *A Study in Scarlet*, the first Holmes story, followed the same monotonous route to publishers taken by his novel *The Firm of Girdlestone*. *Cornhill* magazine rejected it with the chilling comment that it read like a 'shilling dreadful'.

It suffered a similar fate several times over before landing on the desk of a Ward Lock editor in Salisbury Place. The company were looking for material to fill *Beeton's Christmas Annual* for 1887, and a detective story seemed ideally suited to Victorian readers' growing appetite for stirring fiction. Sam Beeton, husband of Isabella, the famous cookery writer, had launched the first-ever Christmas annuals years earlier and, with Ward Lock's marketing, they proved to be a steady seasonal seller. The company, according to practice, offered Doyle £25 to sell the manuscript outright; encouraged by their interest, he decided to press for a royalty. Unfortunately the publisher had heard neither of the Southsea family doctor, nor his rather unusual detective, and replied:

November 2nd 1886

Dear Sir,

In reply to your letter of yesterday's date we regret to say that we shall be unable to allow you to retain a percentage on the sale of your work as it might give rise to some confusion. The tale may have to be inserted together with some other in one of our annuals, therefore we adhere to our original offer of £25 for the complete copyright.

We are, dear Sir,
Yours truly,
Ward, Lock & Co.

*A Study in Scarlet* duly appeared, to a lukewarm reception, alongside columns of trivia, jokes and Christmas puzzles in a volume now so scarce that any new copy to surface is considered a major event in the world of antiquarian books. Only ten are known to be in existence – the British Library, the Bodleian and Cambridge University Library do not have examples – and the last to be sold at auction realized £20,000.

It was, however, *Strand Magazine* which introduced the vast majority of the Holmes stories to the public and made Doyle an international figure. Unlike Ward Lock, where long-term expansion lay in introducing Victorian literature to a wide public, *Strand* was staffed by journalists who reacted quickly to anything which smacked of 'a good read'. Doyle, by this time, had found himself an agent, A. P. Watt, who sent two neatly-written foolscap bundles – *A Scandal in Bohemia* and *The Red-Headed League* – to editor H. Greenhough Smith at the *Strand* offices in Southampton Street. Greenhough Smith, an excitable, impulsive man even in his less enthusiastic moments, felt the adrenalin flow as he read them. He ran the length of proprietor George Newnes's thirty-foot office waving the stories. 'I at

once realized that here was the greatest short-story writer since Edgar Allan Poe', he recalled. 'I remember rushing into the room and thrusting the stories before Mr Newnes's eyes.'

On Doyle's part it was as much a piece of astute salesmanship as masterly writing. Like any conscientious freelance, he had carefully studied the blossoming magazine market and decided that there was a lucrative gap to be filled. 'It struck me', Doyle said later, 'that a single character running through a series – if it engaged the attention of the reader – would bind the reader to that particular magazine. On the other hand, it had long seemed to me that the ordinary serial might be an impediment rather than a help to the magazine since, sooner or later, one missed one number, and

The offices of *Strand* magazine in Southampton Street, London.

afterwards it had lost all interest. Clearly the ideal compromise was a character which carried through in installments which were each complete in themselves ... I believe that I was the first to realize this and *Strand* magazine was the first to put it into practice.'

Lack of patients and a pressing need for money prompted him to settle for Sherlock Holmes. In more relaxed circumstances Doyle might have chosen a different hero set in another age, because he had little regard for the detective story genre. In an interview in 1900 he recalled: 'At the time I first thought of a detective – it was about 1886 – I had been reading some detective stories, and it struck me what nonsense they were, to put it mildly, because for getting the solution of the mystery, the authors always depended on some coincidence. This struck me as not a fair way of playing the game, because the detective ought really to depend for his successes on something in his own mind and not by adventitious circum-

stances which do not, by any means, always occur in real life.'

Doyle's complete restructuring of detective fiction, as we know, paid handsome dividends. Shortly before his death he wrote in the preface to a collection of Holmes stories: '*Study in Scarlet* ... represented a reaction against the too facile way in which the detective of the old school, so far as he was depicted in literature, gained his results. Having endured a severe course of training in medical diagnosis, I felt that if the same austere methods of observation and reasoning were applied to the problems of crime some more scientific system could be constructed. On the whole, taking the series of books, my view has been justified, as I understand that in several countries some change has been made in police procedure on account of these stories.'

Without leaping ahead too far, it was a modest understatement. The Holmes stories were studied with intense interest by police academies in Europe.

H. Greenhough Smith, the editor of *Strand* magazine.

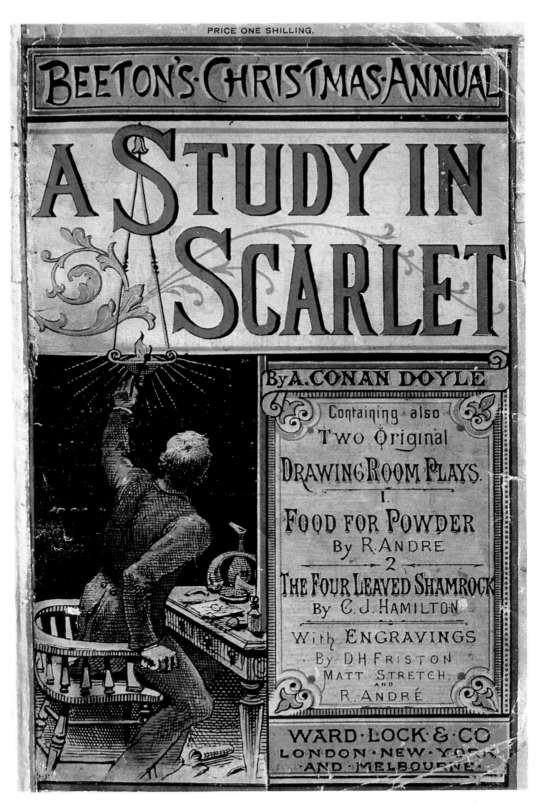

*A Study in Scarlet,* the first Holmes story, was published by Ward Lock in *Beeton's Christmas Annual* 1887.

A colour plate illustration of *The Valley of Fear* from the September 1914 edition of *Strand*.

The original masthead of *Tit-Bits* magazine.

Doyle's weekly postbag, to his increasing dismay, was filled with pleas from all over the world addressed to S. Holmes Esq., begging him to solve cases abandoned as hopeless by the authorities.

As the great age of the novel was taking shape there was a surprising dearth of imaginative, home-grown short stories suitable for the growing magazine market. *Strand*, for instance, had arrived in January 1890 with the bright formula of a picture on every page-spread and, though crammed with lively features, limped along for fiction on translations of Balzac, Hugo and de Maupassant. 'Good story writers were scarce', Greenhough Smith recalled, 'and here, to an editor jaded with wading through reams of impossible stuff, comes a gift from heaven, a godsend in the shape of a story that brought a gleam of happiness into the despairing life of this weary editor. Here was a new and gifted story writer. There was no mistaking the ingenuity of the plot, the limpid clearness of the style, the perfect art of telling a story.'

*Strand* was launched on the profits of *Tit-Bits*, which had achieved a mass circulation in a comparatively short time. Newnes, a draper's representative in Manchester, had conceived the novel idea of starting a magazine full of 'tit-bits of information'. In 1891 the first five thousand copies were snapped up in less than two hours, hawked by brigades of boys in Sam Browne belts and peaked caps with *Tit-Bits* hatbands. When Newnes heard of a pocket of sales resistance in Newcastle because of the saucy-sounding title, he despatched his clergyman brother-in-law on a preaching tour to assure people that it was a respectable publication. Within a year circulation was into six figures and there were twenty-two imitators on the market.

Newnes had a good eye for well-written stories and H. G. Wells, Shaw, P. G. Wodehouse, Somerset Maughan, Galsworthy and Agatha Christie all became regular contributors over the years. Arnold Bennett began his literary career by winning a *Tit-Bits* short-story prize. They rubbed shoulders with a haphazard mixture of

George Newnes, proprietor of *Tit-Bits* and *Strand* magazine.

anecdotes and obscure information: 'The height of Ben Nevis is 4,406 ft. The height of absurdity is not to read *Tit-Bits*', was one of the proprietor's favourite slogans.

The tradition continued in *Strand*, which was aimed at a slightly up-market readership and had less of the terse, dynamic approach of its stablemate. It lacked, however, none of Newnes's unerring sense of what his readers enjoyed. I am the average man', he was fond of saying. 'I don't have to put myself in his place. I am in his place. I know what he wants.' Doyle, the first of the magazine's great fiction contributors, found a welcome niche. He grew fond of the *Strand* and its bright but serious approach, to the point of buying shares in Newnes's company and, later, accepting a seat on the board.

Conan Doyle was offered £200 for the first six Adventures of Sherlock Holmes, which he wrote while keeping his lonely vigil waiting for patients. A turning point in his life came shortly after, when he was laid low by a severe attack of influenza. It began with shivers as he walked to his surgery, and Doyle soon recognized it as the virus which had claimed a disturbing number of lives, including that of his sister Annette. For a week Doyle felt that his life, too, was in the balance. As he lay weak and bedridden he began to think seriously about his future.

Private practice was a precarious profession, dependent on a fickle public impressed with the glib approach and opulent trappings of Wimpole Street. Writing was perhaps an equally risky undertaking but, encouraged by his first earnings and a conviction that he was destined to become a great historical novelist – a dream which was to elude him throughout his career – he grasped the nettle.

'I saw how foolish I was to waste my literary earnings in keeping up an oculist's room in Wimpole Street, and I determined with a wild rush of joy to cut the painter and to trust for ever to my power of writing. I remember in my delight taking the handkerchief which lay upon the coverlet in my enfeebled hand and tossing it up to the ceiling in my exultation. I should at last be my own master. No longer would I have to con-

form to professional dress or try to please anyone else. I would be free to live how I liked and where I liked. It was one of the great moments of exultation of my life.'

The Doyles left the heartless environs of Harley Street and moved to the suburban tranquillity of South Norwood. There he rented a house in Tennison Road – 'a prettily built and modest-looking red-brick residence', according to a *Strand* interviewer – and set up in business as a freelance writer. The decision released the pressures which had mounted with his disenchantment and frustration as a struggling doctor, and the novels and stories began to flow. Unlike many of his contemporaries, he found it easy to write quickly, often delivering works of 40,000 words within two or three months. They arrived at his agent's office in clear, neat script with few alterations or signs of revision.

For both Doyle and Holmes those early days were a prelude to greater things. By Christmas 1890 he was still treading water financially, with little money in the bank as he laboured to build his reputation. *A Study in Scarlet* had attracted less than a flurry of interest and *The Sign of Four*, issued as a book by Spencer Blackett, accumulated cobwebs in the publisher's warehouse. On the bookstalls, however, the stories which were to gather the momentum of a runaway train were selling steadily. In the space of just a year Conan Doyle and his master detective were household names.

As *Strand* ran the Holmes stories *Cornhill* magazine was serializing *The White Company*, a laboured novel set in the fourteenth century. Its acceptance encouraged Doyle to embark on another, *The Refugees*, set in the time of the Huguenots. He scratched away in suburbia unaware and quite unprepared for the vast surge of interest the Holmes stories were generating.

Conan Doyle's study.

When the first series of six drew to a close, Newnes, delighted at the accompanying leap in circulation, offered him £300 for a further six. Doyle, absorbed in the doings of his Huguenot hero, hesitated then reluctantly agreed – on condition that he retained the right to put other literary interests first. At this stage Newnes and Greenhough Smith would have agreed to almost anything to keep their greatest discovery on the *Strand* billboards.

It was the beginning of a long campaign of pressure, cajoling, and heavy persuasion to prise fifty-six Holmes adventures from the unwilling pen of their creator. Before he had even embarked on the second half-dozen, Doyle, infatuated with the idea of honing his historical novels into literary masterpieces, was already secretly laying plans for the death of his detective. With Holmes safely disposed of, he would be able to apply himself completely to the more

*As to my companion neither the country nor the sea presented the slightest attraction to him. He loved to lie in the very centre of five millions of people with his filaments stretching out and running through them, responsive to every little rumour or suspicion of unsolved crime.*

Doyle produced the Holmes stories in a neat handwritten script.

The Holmes adventures evoke an unhurried world of hansom cabs and gaslight.

serious business of novel-writing.

As the fifth *Strand* story was greeted by a stampede for the news-stands, Doyle wrote to his mother revealing that he intended to finish off Holmes in the twelfth tale – the end of his second contract – 'winding him up for good and all... He takes my mind from better things.' His mother, who had longed for the time when her son achieved recognition, was understandably mortified. 'You won't! You can't! You mustn't!' she replied. Like the staff of *Strand* she was aware what an event the first of each month was becoming around the country. But Doyle had underestimated the powerful influence of Newnes, a man used to getting

his own way. Reinforced with Greenhough Smith's infectious enthusiasm, he waged an endless campaign to wear down Doyle's resistance.

In an attempt to duck the second contract the writer had raised his price to £50 a story, but to his dismay Newnes had eagerly agreed. A year later, in February 1892, he was complaining to his mother again: 'They've been bothering me for more Sherlock Holmes tales. Under pressure, I offered to do a dozen for £1000, but I sincerely hope they won't accept it now.' The response from Newnes was a foregone conclusion.

Doyle found the adventures quite

demanding. Their ambling style and ingeniously simple deductions conceal the enormous effort put into their construction. 'The difficulty of the Holmes work', Doyle recalled in his memoirs, 'was that every story really needed as clear-cut and original a plot as a longish book would do. One cannot without effort spin plots at such a rate ...

'At last, after I had done two series of them, I saw that I was in danger of having my hand forced, and of being entirely identified with what I regarded as a lower stratum of literary achievement. Therefore, as a sign of my resolution, I determined to end the life of my hero.'

The detective story, perhaps more than any other fiction form, reflects the mood and pace of the period when it was written. The staccato of Dashiel Hammet mirrors the taut urgency of the inter-war years, just as Holmes's slow deliberations and precise phrasing conjure an unhurried world of hansom cabs and gaslight. Doyle's detective stories are curiously pedantic – this was, after all, the age of popular journalism and publishing for the masses – and one wonders, reading their elegant phrasing, and delightful dialogue, how much Doyle's fixation with the historical novel had overflowed into them.

The stories consumed more of his time as they progressed. Readers became so fascinated by Holmes's deductions that many became completely caught up with the spirit of the stories and challenged some of his methods. In the *Adventure of the Priory School* the detective happens to casually remark that he needed only to glance at a bicycle track on a wet moor to deduce which way it had been travelling. 'I had so many remonstrances on this point', said Doyle, 'that I took out my bicycle and tried. I had imagined that the observations on the

way in which the track of the hind wheel overlaid the track of the front wheel when the machine was not running dead straight would show the direction. I found that my correspondents were right and I was wrong, for this would be the same whichever way the cycle was moving.

'On the other hand, the real solution was much simpler, for on an undulating moor the wheels made a deeper impression uphill and a more shallow one downhill: so Holmes was justified in his wisdom after all.'

Doyle, who had weakened under pressure to write the first twelve stories, eventually succumbed to *Strand*'s silver-tongued persuasion to deliver another dozen. He was clearly unhappy, because in week thirteen no Holmes adventure appeared. Instead, there was a hastily inserted detective story – *The Jewelled Skull* by Dick Donovan – which ended with the triumphant apology: 'It will be observed that this month there is no detective story by Mr Conan Doyle relating the adventures of the celebrated Mr Sherlock Holmes. We are glad to be able to announce that there is to be only a temporary interval in the publication of these stories. Mr Conan Doyle is now engaged upon writing a second series, which will be commenced in an early number.' To keep the interest running an interview with the author was promised, 'containing amongst other interesting matter some particulars concerning Mr Sherlock Holmes'.

Weary and exasperated, Doyle embarked on the adventures which were keeping him from higher things. In the twenty-fourth story he summoned the determination to do what he had long planned, and brought about the end of Sherlock Holmes. Steadily increasing sales of his novel *The White Company*, now in book form, strengthened his resolve. At last his real work was being recognized for its merit. Though, as

Professor Moriarty, 'the Napoleon of Crime'.

Macdonald Hastings, *Strand*'s last editor, remarked, it perhaps never occurred to Doyle that the fame of Sherlock Holmes was boosting the sale of his other books; and without the consulting detective his career might still have been in the doldrums.

The decision lifted a weight from the author's mind; writing the complex Holmes adventures had been a task that rarely came without effort. He had to lock himself in his modest South Norwood study, lined with pictures by his artist father, and think himself into the characters before inspiration

would flow. 'I must admit that in ordinary life I am by no means observant', he commented. 'I have to throw myself into an artificial frame of mind before I can weigh evidence and anticipate the sequence of events.'

The end, of course, had to be a suitably dramatic tribute to the stature Sherlock Holmes had attained. Doyle stumbled on the perfect setting during a short holiday in Switzerland with his wife. As they strolled along the tumbling sweep of the Lauterbrunnen Valley they came to a spot frequented by Victorian tourists – the Reichenbach Falls. 'A terrible place, and one that I thought would make a worthy tomb for poor Sherlock, even if I buried my banking account along with him.' Back in suburbia he sat at his desk with his back to his small cast-iron fire, and wrote the opening lines of *The Final Problem*: 'It is with heavy heart that I take up my pen to write these the last words in which I shall ever record the singular gifts by which my friend Mr Sherlock Holmes was distinguished . . .'

To heighten the enormity of Holmes's demise Doyle arranged for him to be locked in mortal combat with Professor James Moriarty – 'the Napoleon of Crime' – an evil genius who was the elusive godfather of the British underworld. Intellectually, Moriarty was the only worthy opponent for a final denouement. His treatise on the Binomial Theorem had won him a chair in mathematics at a provincial university, until his past caught up with him and 'dark rumours' forced his resignation.

'You have probably never heard of Professor Moriarty?' Holmes asks. 'Never', replies Watson, and in a single word triggered a flurry of intense academic debate. The scheming professor was, in fact, mentioned in *The Valley of Fear* – written after *The Final Solution*, but set *before* the

The struggle between Holmes and Moriarty at Reichenbach Falls.

Reichenbach confrontation. Therefore, technically, Watson did know of Holmes's arch-enemy – but admitting it would have deprived Doyle of a further description of the 'organiser of half that is evil and nearly all that is undetected in this great city'. Such is the microscopic interest in the Holmes adventures that at least two books have been written solely on the problem of the precise dating of *The Valley of Fear*.

As the two grappled on the edge of the falls (where, exactly, on the edge gave rise to another book, *The Final Problem – Where?* by Bryce Crawford and R. C. Moore) they tumbled headlong into the torrent, presumably never to be seen again. (A further volume, by A. Carson Simpson, investigates why the bodies were not fished out downstream by the Swiss police!)

When *The Final Problem* appeared in the December 1893 edition of *Strand*, the re-action was something akin to a national catastrophe. Sackfuls of abusive mail poured into the Southampton Street offices accusing Greenhough Smith of being a disgrace to his profession. Black arm bands were seen on the streets of London and, in the City, brokers tied crêpe bands around their hats. Conan Doyle, expecting to resume his novel writing in peace, received a flood of angry letters, including one from a lady which opened: 'You Brute!'

The author, responsible in the eyes of his readers for an offence equivalent to murdering a national hero, tried to distance himself from the outcry. 'I heard of many who wept', he said. 'I fear I was utterly callous myself and only glad to have a chance of opening out into new fields' ... but with a trace of regret he added, 'The temptation of high prices make it difficult to get one's thoughts away from Holmes.'

As though in a personal warning to Newnes and Greenhough Smith, Doyle had

written at the conclusion of *The Final Problem*: 'Any attempt at recovering the bodies was hopeless, and here, deep down in that dreadful cauldron of swirling water and seething foam, will live for all time the most dangerous criminal and the foremost champion of the law ...' Readers' emotions alternated between anguish and stunned amazement, while Newnes sombrely reported the loss to a meeting of shareholders as 'a dreadful event.' *Strand* no doubt continued to badger Doyle to change his mind, though no records remain of any exchanges between them.

Artist Sidney Paget.

Sidney Paget, the artist who drew the accompanying illustrations, felt a sense of loss, too, for the hero he had clothed and helped to bring to life in the public imagination. Paget was in his early thirties when he first picked up his pen and brushes to illustrate *A Scandal in Bohemia*. In his opening illustration, Holmes, gaunt and with receding hair, stood legs astride before the fire, while a distinguished-looking Dr Watson reclined in a leather armchair. The deerstalker was Paget's invention, and he soon evolved a style in his Holland Park Avenue studio which became familiar to thousands of enthusiasts. Paget, an unassuming man who trained at the Royal Academy School, mulled over various ways of presenting the detective.

He eventually settled on a profile of his brother Walter, who was also an artist. The pale, thin features became so recognizable that Walter once sat down to a Wigmore Hall concert which was disrupted by a woman a few seats away calling: 'Why, there's Sherlock Holmes!'

The great detective may have been somewhere in the 'swirling water and seething foam' of the Reichenbach Falls, but it was clear he was not going to rest in peace.

Doyle continued to receive letters from *Strand* readers who had already bombarded him with requests for Holmes's or Watson's autograph. Ladies offered to keep house for the distinguished bachelor sleuth – one even adding the recommendation that she understood beekeeping. Even a press-clipping agency, touting for business, tried to solicit Holmes as a client. Despite the obviously great public affection for his hero, Doyle continued to have little regard for him.

In his last interview, for the *Evening News* just two months before his death, he was still trying to forget his greatest creation. 'I have done with him', he said. 'To tell the truth I am rather tired of hearing myself described as the author of Sherlock Holmes.

An illustration from *The Silver Blaze*. Holmes's famous deerstalker was Paget's invention.

An illustration from Conan Doyle's historical novel, *Brigadier Gerard*.

Why not, for a change, the author of *Rodney Stone*, or *The White Company*, or *Brigadier Gerard*, or of *The Lost World*? One would think I had written nothing but detective stories.'

Sir Arthur, as he had become, was already weak and ailing and had been forced to cancel all social engagements. 'You know', he told the reporter as they sat together in his Crowborough study, 'what strikes me most in growing old is how little one changes. If I sit down and close my eyes I feel little change since my early middle age. I have the same sentiments, the same enthusiasms, much the same convictions. I hope I may have gained a little wisdom, if I have less energy.'

The great sportsman and adventurer had slowed considerably. Holmes, he felt, had cheated him of greater recognition. But, tired though he was of his irritatingly durable detective, Conan Doyle suddenly stirred with interest and enthusiasm towards the end of the conversation. 'On hearing the question "Was there a Sherlock Holmes in real life?" Sir Arthur sat upright in his armchair. "Most certainly there was", he said. "He was a doctor in Edinburgh – a Dr Bell – under whom I studied. He had an almost uncanny gift for drawing large inferences from small observations. When I tried to draw a detective I naturally thought of Dr Bell and his methods, and what he applied to the diagnosis of disease I applied to the diagnosis of crime."'

Much has been written of Dr Joe Bell, Doyle's white-haired gimlet-eyed tutor at Edinburgh Royal Infirmary, and scholarly arguments continue to sail back and forth as to how much of him there was in Sherlock Holmes. Scientific method in police work was in its infancy at the time, and largely in the hands of a few gifted pathologists and police surgeons. Doyle, in building the character of his detective, needed to lift him above the facile plodders of Victorian crime fiction and imbue him with the authority of scientific method. And what could have been more natural at this point than for his thoughts to drift back to Dr Bell and his extraordinary diagnostic technique.

Bell, a Presbyterian Scot with a dry sense of humour, would sit in his consulting-room, steepling his fingers like Holmes, flanked by a semi-circle of students. When a patient was ushered in his bright, sharp eyes would rake him and, before they could utter a word, Bell would come out with an astutely-observed deduction:

Dr Joseph Bell, Doyle's medical tutor, was 'the original of Sherlock Holmes'.

'Well, my man, you've served in the army.'

'Aye, Sir.'

'Not long discharged?'

'No, Sir.'

'A Highland Regiment?'

'Aye, Sir.'

'A non-commissioned officer.'

'Aye, Sir.'

'Stationed at Barbados.'

'Aye, Sir.'

When the patient had left after his examination, Bell would turn to his students and explain: 'You see, gentlemen, the man was a respectful man but did not remove his hat. They do not in the army, but he would have learned civilian ways had he long been discharged. He has an air of authority and he is obviously Scottish. As to Barbados, his complaint is elephantiasis, which is West Indian, and not British.'

Conan Doyle the medical student was Bell's Watson, incredulous and impressed, as they all were, at his diagnostic technique; and, according to contemporaries, busily writing down every word his tutor spoke. 'It is no wonder that after the study of such a character I used and amplified his methods when in later life I tried to build up a scientific detective who solved cases on his own merits.' It is no surprise that years later, in *The Greek Interpreter*, we encounter Watson, Holmes and the detective's civil servant brother, Mycroft, sitting in the window of the Diogenes Club, surveying the passing scene in Pall Mall.

'An old soldier, I perceive,' said Sherlock.

'And very recently discharged,' said the older brother.

'Served in India, I see.'

'And a non-commissioned officer.'

'Royal Artillery, I fancy,' said Sherlock.

'And a widower.'

Lord Baden-Powell was one of many who experienced the Bell method at first hand. In *Scouting for Boys* he recalled Bell asking a student what was wrong with a patient who had been led into the surgery. The hapless student admitted that he did not know because he had not asked him. 'Well there is no need to ask him', the doctor replied. 'You should see for yourself – he has injured his right knee – he is limping on that leg; he injured it by burning it in the fire. You see how his trouser leg is burnt away at the knee. This is Monday morning, yesterday was fine; Saturday was wet and muddy. The man's trousers are muddy all over. He had a fall in the mud on Saturday night.' Then, turning to the patient, he said: 'You drew your wages Saturday and got drunk, and in trying to get your clothes dry by the fire when you got home, you fell on the fire and burnt your knee – isn't that so!'

'Yes, Sir', replied the amazed man.

Half way through the second dozen Holmes adventures, George Newnes despatched his best reporter, Harry How, to Conan Doyle's suburban semi to write a profile on the great man at home. Doyle was photographed in tweed cap and plus-fours, perched on a tandem with his wife. ('He is never happier than when starting a thirty-mile spin ...'). After a tour of the house they settled down to tea ('The chairs are cosy and the thin bread and butter delicious ...') while Doyle talked a little more about his tutor. He had acted as Bell's ward clerk, rounding up seventy or eighty patients at a time for consultation, and jotting down notes on their condition.

'Case number one would step up. "I see", said Mr Bell, "you're suffering from drink. You even carry a flask in the inside breast pocket of your coat."

'Another case would come forward. "Cobbler, I see." Then he would turn to the students and point out to them that the

Sherlock Holmes, like Dr Bell in his consulting room, would sit steepling his
fingers as he quietly observed his clients.

inside of the knee of the man's trousers was
worn. That was where the man had rested
the lapstone – a peculiarity only found in
cobblers. All this impressed me very much.
He was continually before me – his sharp,
piercing grey eyes, eagle nose and striking
features. There he would sit in his chair
with fingers together – he was very dexter-
ous with his hands – and just look at the
man or woman before him. He was most
kind and painstaking with the students – a
real good friend. The remarkable individuality and discriminating tact of my old
master made a deep and lasting impression
on me, though I had not the faintest idea
that it would one day lead me to forsake
medicine for story writing.'

The Method itself was not unique. Vol-
taire's Zadig 'acquired a perspicacity which
showed him a thousand differences where
other men see only uniformity'. When the
King of Babylon's horse bolts he examines
the tracks: 'The dust on the trees in this
narrow road only seven feet wide was raised

a little right and left, three and a half feet
from the middle of the road. This horse,
said I, has a tail three and a half feet long,
and its movement right and left has swept
up this dust. I saw beneath the trees which
made a cradle five feet high, some leaves
newly fallen from the branches, and I
recognized that this horse had touched
there, and was hence fifteen hands high. As
regards his bit, it must be of twenty-three
carat gold, for he rubbed the studs against a
stone, which I know to be a touchstone and
tested. From the marks his hoofs made on
certain pebbles I knew the horse was shod
with eleven scruple silver.'

Holmes's first meeting with Watson in *A
Study in Scarlet* – 'You've been to Afghanistan, I perceive' – had distant echoes, too, in
*Monsieur Lecoq*, the detective hero of
French writer Emile Gaboriau. Doyle
admired the 'neat dovetailing of his plots',
but there was an abundance of slick deduction in the stories, too. Lecoq may have
lacked the formidable intellect of Holmes,

but the technique was familiar. One glance at a footprint by lantern light and he explains: 'He was standing on tiptoe with outstretched neck and listening ears, when, on reaching this spot he heard some noise; fear seized him and he fled . . .'

Unlike Doyle, who had studiously followed Wilkie Collins's Sergeant Cuff in *The Moonstone* and Edgar Allen Poe's Detective Dupin, Bell was an original. A true exponent – possibly the only living one – of the scientific method of inspired deduction. 'You know my method – it is founded upon held close to the cheek while smoking – the characteristic attitude of the peasant woman smoking a clay pipe as she sits by her fireplace.'

Dr Bell was not, however, completely ignorant of detective fiction. 'Every book-stall has its shilling shocker, and every magazine which aims at a circulation must have its mystery of robbery or murder,' he wrote in a preface to *A Study in Scarlet*. 'Most of these are poor stuff; complicated plots which can be discounted in the first chapter, extraordinary coincidences,

Holmes practises the Method in *The Yellow Face*. The owner of the pipe is, he concludes, 'obviously a muscular man, left-handed, with an excellent set of teeth, careless in his habits and with no need to practise economy.'

the observation of trifles,' says Holmes in the *Boscombe Valley Mystery*, mirroring Dr Bell's approach perfectly. One former student, Dr J. Gordon Wilson, fondly remembered an old lady being shown in and, to everyone's amazement, Bell asking her where her tobacco pipe was. 'Did you notice the ulcer on her lower lip and the glossy scar on her left cheek indicating a superficial burn?' he asked them later. 'All marks of a short-stemmed clay pipe preternaturally gifted detectives who make discoveries more or less useless by flashes of insight which no one else can understand, become wearisome in their sameness; the interest, such as it is, centres only in the results and not in the methods.'

Bell's detective work was put to wider use when Edinburgh police called him out to help with scene-of-crime investigations. His keen observation led him to appear as a prosecution witness, giving evidence which secured many convictions. It was inevitable, then, that a series of unsolved murders three hundred miles away in London should attract his attention. In 1888 swirling mists from the eastern reaches of the Thames cloaked the identity of Jack the Ripper, who haunted the narrow cobbled alleys of Whitechapel. For four months he terrorized the district with seven street murders, precipitating enormous public reaction. Thousands poured into Whitechapel to gaze morbidly at the scene of the crimes until police reinforcements had to be drafted into the notorious square mile.

Local residents formed vigilante committees to patrol the gas-lit courts and foggy lanes, but he continued to outwit them, stabbing and dissecting his women victims with fiendish delight. Police tacked rubber strips to their boots to patrol silently. More than a thousand suspects were hauled in for interrogation and, before the killings came to an abrupt halt in November, theories were swirling like autumn leaves in the wind. The mutilations suggested someone with a knowledge of anatomy, and the mad doctor theory was popular for a while. Others claimed that he worked on a cattle boat, because crimes coincided with vessels berthing in the East End docks from the north of England.

Newspapers boosted their circulations by suggesting new suspects – the *Star*'s figures rocketed from 100,000 to a quarter of a million when it named an innocent Polish immigrant. When he finally established his alibi, chief reporter Kennedy Jones and his news team became understandably twitchy. Only some extremely supple legal gymnastics enabled them to escape with £50 libel costs; they were bracing themselves for £5,000. As another newspaper pointed the finger at a member of the Metropolitan Police, the *Star* got its second

wind and plunged after a Home Counties horticulturalist, also innocent. Mercifully for the newspaper, if not the poor man's horrified family, he was found drowned in the Thames.

The passage of time has done little to diminish the tangle of loose ends and speculation. There have been suggestions that the Ripper was the Duke of Clarence, who was 'restrained in a mental home' and the whole affair hushed up. The author overlooked the fact that the Duke was still happily making public appearances four years after the murders. There was even a Jill the Ripper theory that only a woman – obviously a midwife crazed with bloodlust – could walk undetected through such heavily-patrolled streets. Masonic ritual killings were another fashionable favourite. While some made up in book sales what they lacked in conviction, Jack would probably have laughed up his sleeve, as he did at the overworked police trying to bring him to justice. He would take a ginger beer bottle to the scene of a murder, fill it with half a pint of blood and, once safely home, use it to write to the press and police.

Dear Boss,
    Grand work that last job was. I gave the lady no time to squeal. I love my work and want to start again. The next job I do I shall clip the lady's ear off. Good luck.
    Yours truly,
    Jack the Ripper.
P.S. They say I'm a doctor now. Ha, Ha.

Seldom had such a sensational and challenging case come the way of police already hardened to a growing catalogue of East End crime. It was perfect material for Dr Bell – Holmes, too, had he been on the scene – and he set about it with great enthusiasm.

With the help of a friend who shared his interest in the case, Bell closely examined Scotland Yard's handful of major suspects and several of his own. A joint approach to solving the killings was part of his strategy. 'When two men set out to find a golf ball in the rough', he told the *Edinburgh Evening News*, 'they expect to come across it where the straight line, marked in their minds' eye from their original positions, crossed. In the same way, when two men set out to investigate a crime mystery, it is where their researches intersect that we have a result.' And have a result he did, but sadly the name of Bell's suspect was never published. According to Bell's biographer, Professor Ely Liebow, both the doctor and his friend arrived at their separate conclusions, wrote down the name of the man they suspected and exchanged pieces of paper. When they found that the names were identical they immediately contacted officers investigating the Ripper case. Curiously, says Liebow, the murders came to an abrupt end a week later. Coincidence – or perhaps the most dramatic proof of the efficacy of the Method?

Doyle had a varied life before crossing paths with Dr Bell. He came from a family of artists: John Doyle, famous to Victorians as H. B., the caricaturist, was his grandfather. He drew 'gentlemen for gentlemen' with a wit and whiff of satire which made him immensely popular. Doyle's uncle, Dicky Doyle, found a home for his impish brand of humour in *Punch*, where he designed the magazine's original masthead. Conan Doyle's father, Charles, by comparison was an impoverished civil service clerk in Edinburgh's Department of Works. In his spare time he painted haunting, whimsical pictures from the impoverished surroundings of their Georgian terrace in Picardy Place. Like her husband, Conan Doyle's mother, Mary, was of Irish descent, with a wiry determination to do the best she could for her family. Like many poor women her will to see him succeed was driven in inverse proportion to her income. The more the family struggled for money, the greater effort she put into turning them out warm, well fed, scrubbed and bright as new buttons. Doyle developed into a tough schoolboy who invariably came home dishevelled and dirty from fighting. Later, as his goals became those of the rising middle classes, he channelled his aggression into boxing, rugby and a love of any sport with contact and spills. While Watson was never to inherit the roguish humour of the artist Doyles – he was never over-endowed with a sense of fun – Holmes acquired his creator's passion for boxing and physical activity. Lesser boys than Doyle had been broken by the harsh regime of punishment and physical training at Stoneyhurst Jesuit college, near Preston, which he attended from the age of nine. He endured Latin and Greek in a spartan atmosphere of cold baths and hard discipline, rising to edit the school magazine in the time-honoured manner of many a literary rebel.

Doyle left at sixteen with the sobering prophecy of one of his Jesuit masters ringing in his head: 'Doyle, I have known you now for seven years, and I know you thoroughly. I am going to say something which you will remember in after-life. Doyle – you will never come to any good.'

The determined Mrs Doyle, however, thought otherwise. Charles, though still bringing home his meagre £240 a year (£300 was Mrs Beeton's lowest estimate to run an average middle-class household), had drifted away from earthly cares to lose himself almost entirely in his dreamlike paintings. His apparent indifference galvanized Mary into scraping together

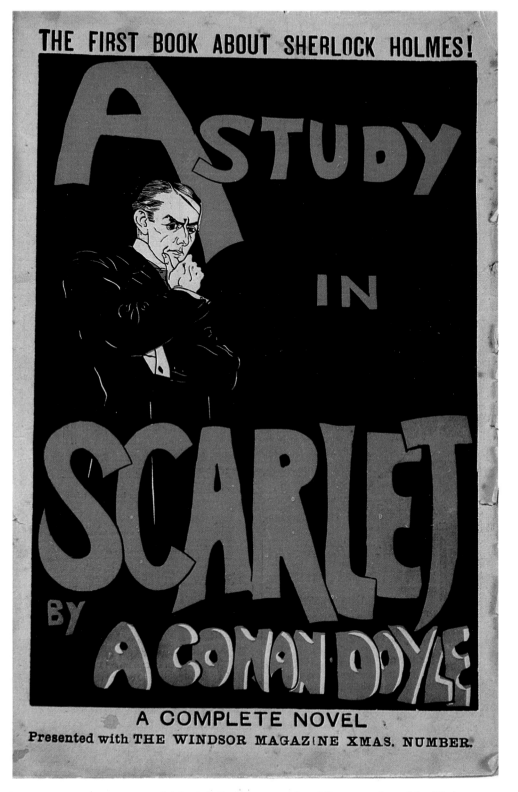

THE FIRST BOOK ABOUT SHERLOCK HOLMES!

A STUDY

IN

SCARLET

BY A CONAN DOYLE

A COMPLETE NOVEL

Presented with THE WINDSOR MAGAZINE XMAS. NUMBER.

In 1895 a paperback copy of *A Study in Scarlet* was presented free to readers of the Christmas edition of the *Windsor Magazine*.

SIR NIGEL

is the hero of Sir A. Conan Doyle's stirring new serial
which commences in the December Xmas Double Number of the "Strand Magazine." The above picture
illustrates a thrilling incident in the first instalment.

STRAND MAGAZINE

This colour illustration advertised the forthcoming serialization of Conan Doyle's historical
novel, *Sir Nigel*, in *Strand* magazine.

Age 4

Age 14

Age 22

Age 32

A. Conan Doyle (1859–1930).

enough money to send Conan to Edinburgh University to study medicine.

Doyle took to the course with the bravura he displayed on the rugby field, and the eager devotion he applied to reading. Books were so important to him that he would forego his lunch and spend the money on Pope, Poe and Oliver Wendell Holmes, after whom he was to name his great detective.

The university, where Doyle encountered the remarkable Dr Bell, provided influences which shaped his literary career. If Bell was his sun, lighting up a gruelling study course with wit and intellect, Doyle encountered his dark moon in the form of a wildly eccentric, highly gifted, but completely anarchic fellow-student named George Budd. According to Doyle's biographer, Hesketh Pearson, Budd had 'a bulldog jaw, over-hanging brows, small, deep-set, light blue bloodshot eyes, set close together and either radiating geniality or darting forth gleams of diabolical hatred ... He was half-genius, half-maniac with a streak of charlatanism in his genius and some sense in his mania'.

Budd invited Doyle to join him in a chaotic medical practice in Plymouth, only, in an act of revenge, to force him into disas-trous financial circumstances. The out-come, for which we must be grateful, was that the almost destitute Conan Doyle was forced to spend more time writing while waiting for non-existent patients to file into his empty surgery. Doyle the young doctor was entranced and slightly mesmerized by the erratic Budd, whose lifestyle seemed free from all the disciplines of Stoneyhurst and constraints of poverty in Picardy Place. Budd swung wildly from inventing bizarre devices – magnets to draw away enemy shells, mechanical plugs to save holed ships, patent blood tonic – to courting publicity in a most desperate fashion.

Against a stream of advice from his mother, Doyle accepted the offer to join Budd in practice. Level-headed Mary was seldom wrong when it came to guiding her son's fortunes (it was she, after all, who pleaded with him not to kill off Holmes), and she insisted that he brake off the partnership. Doyle was so spellbound by his powerful Nemesis that it was the only occasion over which there was real conten-tion between them.

Budd laid on extravagant performances for his patients, treating them in a flam-boyant, cavalier manner which overturned any notion of medical ethics drummed into them as students. The more he stepped-up his crude salesmanship – treatment was

free, patients paid only for the medicine – the longer the queue outside his surgery grew. Doyle, a rumbustious young man who nevertheless took his calling seriously, could barely compete in his tiny room across the corridor. Budd was preoccupied with making his fortune at the expense of Plymouth's fashionable, but staid, family doctors; and rather than turn business away, he hoped to use Doyle to increase his practice further.

Budd dispensed hearty slaps, placebos, threats and flattery but, predictably, the novelty wore off and patients began to drift back in ones and twos to the more peaceful waiting rooms of their former GPs. Budd accused his more courteous partner of caus-ing business to slide, and the first sign of his volatile acrimony began to surface. Behind all his drunken brawls, patent medicines and blatant showmanship Budd showed flashes of rare genius. Even at medical school he had amazed everyone by emerg-ing from a wild spree to win the coveted anatomy prize effortlessly.

Conan Doyle the writer, in creating Professor James Moriarty, the arch example of a brilliant mind gone wrong, perhaps recalled the emotional bruising of his brush with Dr Budd. Their relationship deterior-ated when Budd and his wife began secretly rifling Doyle's pockets when he had retired to bed, and discovered Mary's outspoken letters. Unable to reveal that they had read them, they rounded on the hapless Doyle and, by accusing him of ruining the prac-tice, manoeuvred him into offering to resign. Before he had the opportunity to leave, Budd fell ill with rheumatic fever, at which Doyle generously offered to take over his patients until he recovered. The Budds ungraciously insisted on paying to under-line their feelings.

A few weeks later Doyle departed on a

steamer for Portsmouth, feeling understandably confused, with little more than a trunk, his brass name-plate, a stethoscope and six pounds. There he took lodgings and set out to look for an area where property might be cheap and patients plentiful. He eventually settled on Bush Villa, a red-brick house with an iron gate in unpretentious Southsea where, four years later, he was to write *A Study in Scarlet*. Somehow he contrived to make it look furnished, with a curtain draped across the hall to conceal the bareness beyond. What few items he could afford were spread thinly, but with extreme care, across the consulting room and lobby,

to suggest a comfort which was beyond his means.

Only the hope of his long-overdue £20 fee arriving from the Budds sustained him through this period of austerity. To maintain his carefully cultivated veneer of middle class stability he secretly gave up cigarettes and survived on a diet of bread and sausages. Even his long-running correspondence with his mother occasionally had to be suspended because of the price of a stamp. Somewhat predictably the Budd's promised money never arrived. In its place came a letter denouncing him as a traitor to their friendship. They claimed to have

Victorian Plymouth, where Doyle shared a medical practice with Budd.

found a letter from Mary Doyle describing his former partner as a 'bankrupt swindler'. Mrs Doyle, as usual, had accurately summed up the situation. Doyle's initial feelings of wounded betrayal gave way to a sense of relief as he faced a fresh start away from the paranoic atmosphere of Plymouth. Budd may have gained the impression that his partner was easily manipulated and incapable of surviving without his patronage, but he underestimated Doyle's deep resources. Unlike Budd, he was a stranger to self-indulgence and saw a challenge in adversity. In his last year at Edinburgh he had signed on as a ship's surgeon on a tough, ocean-going whaler, where he fought bare-fisted and earned the respect and friendship of the seasoned crew. In sedate Southsea, as in the Arctic, Doyle's buoyant spirit was undiminished, and he used the episode to enrich his experience.

Hesketh Pearson, and others, believed that the misalliance 'left its trace in his writings, which are peppered with blackguards whose behaviour has the same groundless and nightmare quality'. Indeed, by 1901 he had clearly not forgotten the malevolent Dr Budd. Doyle submitted a series of three articles for *Strand* entitled 'Strange Studies From Life'. In one of them he reflects upon the story of William Godfrey Youngman, hanged in 1860 for stabbing his mother and two small brothers.

'In the study of criminal psychology,' Doyle wrote, 'one is forced to the conclusion that the most dangerous of all types of mind

By the turn of the century *Strand*'s high-speed presses could barely keep pace with the public's demand for the increasingly popular magazine.

is that of the inordinately selfish man. He is a man who has lost his sense of proportion. His own will and his own interest have blotted out for him the duty which he owes to the community ... The player who makes the mistake of selfishness may have a terrible forfeit to pay – but the unaccountable thing in the rules is that some, who are only spectators of his game, may have to help him in the paying.'

Throughout the 1890s Conan Doyle continued to write for *Strand* which, thanks to the initial thrust of the Holmes adventures, was enjoying a half-million circulation in 1896. By the turn of the century Newnes's skilful management of its contents prompted one traveller on the boat train from Waterloo to Southampton to note that 'every other person on the train had a copy'. Doyle had followed its progress from the first issue and developed a great affection for its policy of 'information as entertainment', and bringing quality reading to the masses. Although he remained on amicable terms with Newnes and Greenhough Smith, he preferred the social life of his friend Jerome K. Jerome's *Idler* magazine, where he batted for the cricket XI. On returning from a trip to Europe he wrote to a friend: 'Foreigners used to recognise the English by their check suits. I think they will soon learn to do it by their *Strand* magazines. Everyone on the Channel boat, except the man at the wheel, was clutching one.'

Eventually – perhaps inevitably – he was drawn to resurrecting Holmes. His reasons are unclear; by 1901 his novels had achieved moderate success, enough at least to relieve him of financial pressure and, in some ways, there was less reason than ever to bring his national hero back to life. But with almost a decade in which to pursue his prime interests, and the irritation at letters

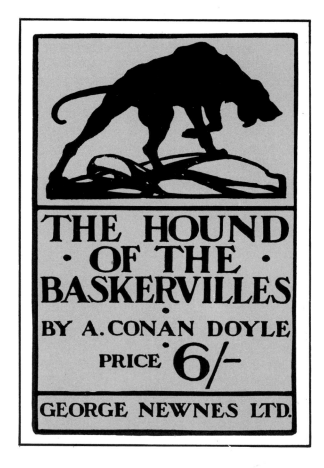

The Strand serialization of *The Hound of the Baskervilles* boosted circulation to 30,000 a month.

addressed to S. Holmes Esq. soothed by the passage of time, he was ready to meet his creation face to face again. The intervening years had also given Doyle time to adjust to the acclaim which greeted each Holmes story. He was finally beginning to accept, if not entirely approve of, the great detective, and perhaps in a small degree even missed him. Throughout the 1890s Newnes had paid him handsomely for his contributions , never less than £100 for a thousand words.

Frustrated followers had kept the Holmes

flame alive throughout the years of deprivation by banding together in American cities. His whole life was already being venerated and the stories dissected and analysed with an intensity previously enjoyed only by the Bible. There was a surge of adrenalin when *Strand* hysterically billed THE REAPPEARANCE OF SHERLOCK HOLMES in the form of a serial called *The Hound of the Baskervilles*. It was a long, self-contained reminiscence, carefully set before Holmes's disappearance so that there could be no question of a come-back.

A naive visitor wandering down Southampton Street might have been forgiven for mistaking *Strand*'s offices for the opening of the Oxford Street summer sales. A long queue snaked around the building, waiting to buy copies directly across the mahogany counter of the front office. Each instalment, for which Doyle was paid between £460 and £680 according to length, boosted circulation by 30,000 a month. There was clearly a mood among readers of jubilant elation.

Conan Doyle, a modest, genial man to all who recalled him, had nevertheless displayed a touch of that common affliction, fiction-writer's arrogance, since he first picked up the pen. Early stirrings of academic interest in the Holmes stories confirmed his conviction that he had elevated the detective story to a higher form. If he was flattered by the attention, he would almost certainly have been exasperated and embarrassed at the later microscopic fixation with his work. Something – public reaction, intellectual acclaim, breathtakingly high fees – began to send the first hair-line cracks of doubt through his resolve. By the time the second instalment of *The Hound of the Baskervilles* was being torn from the news-stands, he was hesitantly saying in a *Harper*'s interview; 'I know that my friend Dr Watson is a most trustworthy man, and I give the utmost credit to his story of the dreadful affair in Switzerland. He may have been mistaken, of course. It may not have been Mr Holmes who fell from the ledge at all . . .'

The article presumably did not escape the attention of Newnes, by then Sir George. Although *The Hound of the Baskervilles* was a tremendous publishing success, it was clear that the gnawing hunger of Holmes's public would not be satiated by mere retrospectives. Nothing short of the great man being found alive and well and back in Baker Street, mulling over new three-pipe problems, would suffice. Poor Doyle could not fight the whole British public; to say nothing of an army of eager readers across the world waiting for the decision he was being inexorably manoeuvred into making.

Two years later, in September 1903, a display advertisement in *Strand* shrilled: 'THE RETURN OF SHERLOCK HOLMES – Readers have a vivid recollection of the time when Sherlock Holmes made his first appearance before the public, and of the Adventures which made his name a household word in every quarter of the world. The news of his death was received with regret as at the loss of a personal friend. Fortunately, the news, though based on circumstantial evidence which at the time seemed conclusive, turns out to be erroneous. How he escaped from his struggle with Moriarty at the Reichenbach Falls, why he remained in hiding even from his friend Watson, how he made his reappearance, and the manner he signalised his return by one of the most remarkable of his exploits will be found in the first story of the New Series, beginning in the October Number.'

There was pandemonium when *The Adventure of the Empty House* appeared four

# THE RETURN

## OF

# SHERLOCK HOLMES.

## By A. CONAN DOYLE.

The Readers of

## THE 'STRAND MAGAZINE'

have a vivid recollection of the time when Sherlock Holmes made his first appearance before the public, and of the Adventures which made his name a household word in every quarter of the world.

### THE NEWS OF HIS DEATH

was received with regret as at the loss of a personal friend. Fortunately, that news, though based on circumstantial evidence which at the time seemed conclusive,

### TURNS OUT TO BE ERRONEOUS.

How he escaped from his struggle with Moriarty at the Reichenbach Falls,

### WHY HE REMAINED IN HIDING

even from his friend Watson, how he made his re-appearance, and the manner he signalised his return by one of the

### MOST REMARKABLE OF HIS EXPLOITS,

will be found narrated in the first story of the New Series beginning in the

### OCTOBER NUMBER.

READY THURSDAY, OCTOBER 1. PRICE 6d.

B

9

September 1903: *Strand* advertises the return
of Sherlock Holmes.

weeks later. Those who read, and were to re-read, every word must have nodded in fond satisfaction at Watson's account of why the old fox had astutely gone to ground. There was finally no doubt that, as Holmes would have remarked: 'The game's afoot again, Watson.'

Doyle was well compensated for his reluctant return to the claustrophobic confines of 221B Baker Street. For the American rights alone he was paid $5,000 – a record for the time – for each of the thirteen episodes.

Newnes, who used to invite visitors to watch his high-speed *Tit-Bits* and *Strand* presses in action, found that the technology of the age was overtaken by demand. Despondent readers who could not obtain copies queued at public libraries, which obligingly extended reading-room opening hours on publication day each month.

The popularity and feverish response to the return of Holmes was a curious phenomenon, explained partly by the trauma of the new century. It was with great reluctance that people slipped the comforting ties of the Victorian era and slid into an age of uncertainty, already overcast with dark clouds from Europe. The first, long-awaited stride into the twentieth century became a tentative step into the unknown. Brooding social unrest, German military posturing, and inventions which seemed certain to destroy traditional patterns, created a timid yearning for old values and familiar friends.

'It was as if they unconsciously resented the new era, dreading its hidden possibilities, and longed to return to the saner and safer past', Reginald Pound observed in his history of *Strand Magazine*. 'For them it was only yesterday and already it had an easeful period charm that could be savoured again ...' The passing of time was to bring new troubles which drew deeper yearnings for

the cosy, twilight of late Victorian days. By the 1930s, when history seemed likely to repeat itself, Edgar W. Smith was waxing biblically in the *Baker Street Journal* about 'the half-remembered, half-forgotten times of snug Victorian illusion, of gaslit comfort and contentment, of perfect dignity and grace ... We love the place in which the Master moved and had his being: the England of those times, fat with the fruits of her achievements, but strong and daring still with the spirit of imperial adventure.'

Holmes's absence for almost three years following the Reichenbach Falls incident – known in Sherlockian circles as the Great Hiatus – was spent in Tibet with the head lama, in the Middle East where he 'looked in on Mecca', and in research into coal-tar derivatives at a laboratory in Montpelier. He hastened home only when Moriarty's henchmen were dealt with, to look into the Park Lane murder of the Hon. Ronald Adair. Mrs Hudson, the housekeeper, understandably had hysterics when he walked into 221B again. And while it may have seemed unkind not to confide in the loyal and trustworthy Watson, readers accepted the explanation magnanimously, relieved and grateful that he had returned at all.

Doyle's hefty fees for the resumed Holmes stories did little to cushion him from the mail once more pouring into his home, incredible though some of the letters were – bearing gifts of tobacco, spare violin strings and packets of pipe cleaners. There were appeals to trace missing wills, lost relatives, stolen jewelry and all the old requests for photographs, autographs and mementoes of Baker Street's most famous resident.

'I do not think that I ever realised what a living, actual personality Holmes had become to the more guileless readers until I heard of the very pleasing story of the char-à-bancs of French schoolboys who, when asked what they wanted to see first in London, replied unanimously that they wanted to see Mr Holmes's lodgings in Baker Street. Many have asked me which house it is, but that is a point which for excellent reasons I will not decide . . .'

Among the 'guileless readers' was the Turkish government which, according to a *Times* foreign correspondent, suspected Sherlock Holmes of slipping into their country as an agent for the Foreign Office.

In Cairo, police cadets studied the adventures, translated into Arabic, as part of their training course. Germans embraced a new word into the language, '*sherlockieren*', to deduce, or run to ground.

The faithful had been sustained throughout the lean years by a stage play, *Sherlock Holmes*, stitched together from three different plots by an enthusiastic American, William Gillette, who also played the title role. He had the courtesy to bring the final draft to London personally for Conan

The American actor William Gillette was responsible for the introduction of the famous drooping Holmesian pipe.

Holmes tackles the snake in *The Speckled Band*.

Doyle's blessing. According to one account Gillette, anxious to ingratiate himself, stepped from the train in deerstalker and Holmesian caped overcoat to shake hands with the rather glazed author. After a successful American tour the play opened to packed houses at the Lyceum, followed by a capacity provincial tour which continued until the *Strand* serialization of *Hound of the Baskervilles* finished. Gillette, incidentally, was responsible for the famous drooping Holmesian pipe; he found it impossible to speak his lines with his teeth clamped on a straight briar.

The production helped to create the climate for the epidemic of Holmes fever which accompanied the return of the stories. Doyle entered further into the spirit of the phenomenon by writing his own stage play based on *The Speckled Band*. 'When I saw the course that things were taking I shut myself up and devoted my whole mind to making a sensational Holmes drama', Conan Doyle recalled. His prodigious story output – 3,000 words a day in immaculate handwriting were a leisurely stroll – adapted easily to writing a play. Within a week the script was ready for rehearsal at the Royal Adelphi in 1910.

He was pleased with the cast – the distinguished H. A. Saintsbury as Holmes and Lyn Harding as the formidable Dr Grimesby Rycott – but the production also hinged on the acting prowess of a four-foot snake, which caused endless problems. 'We had several snakes at different times', said Doyle, 'but they were none of them born actors and they were all inclined to hang down from the hole in the wall like inanimate bell-pulls, or else to turn back through the hole and get even with the stage carpenter who pinched their tails in order to make them more lively.' The finest of them, a magnificent rock boa, behaved impeccably, only to be panned by the critics as 'a palpably artificial serpent'. Finally the producer resorted to rubber dummies with great success.

*The Speckled Band* proved very profitable and created greater interest in the Holmes adventures. Studies of the Works by afficionados became so deeply serious, particularly after Doyle's death, that it is refreshing to note that among his treasured mementoes was 'a rollocking parady' of Holmes and Watson, written by Sir James Barrie to cheer him up after an unsuccessful joint effort to produce a comic opera. It is wickedly witty and seldom seen. I make no excuse for reproducing it as a hearty antidote to the plethora of studies – academic and pseudo-academic – on the subject:

## The Adventure of the Two Collaborators

IN BRINGING TO a close the adventures of my friend Sherlock Holmes I am perforce reminded that he never, save on the occasion which, as you will now hear, brought his singular career to an end, consented to act in any mystery which was concerned with persons who made a livelihood by their pen.

'I am not particular about the people I mix among for business purposes', he would say, 'but at literary characters I draw the line.'

We were in our rooms in Baker Street one evening. I was (I remember) by the centre table writing out 'The Adventure of the Man Without a Cork Leg' (which had so puzzled the Royal Society and all the other scientific bodies of Europe), and Holmes was amusing himself with a little revolver

practice. It was his custom of a summer evening to fire round my head, just shaving my face, until he had made a photograph of me on the opposite wall, and it is a slight proof of his skill that many of these portraits in pistol shots are considered admirable likenesses.

I happened to look out of the window, and, perceiving two gentlemen advancing rapidly along Baker Street, asked him who they were. He immediately lit his pipe, and, twisting himself on a chair into the figure 8, replied: 'They are two collaborators in comic opera, and their play has not been a triumph.'

I sprang from my chair to the ceiling in amazement, and then he explained: 'My dear Watson, they are obviously men who follow some low calling. That much even you should be able to read in their faces. Those little pieces of blue paper which they fling angrily from them are Durrant's Press Notices. Of these they have obviously hundreds about their person (see how their pockets bulge). They would not dance on them if they were pleasant reading.'

I again sprang to the ceiling (which is much dented) and shouted: 'Amazing! But they may be mere authors.'

'No,' said Holmes, 'for mere authors get only one Press notice a week. Only criminals, dramatists and actors get them by the hundred.'

'Then they may be actors.'

'No; actors would come in a carriage.'

'Can you tell me anything else about them?'

'A great deal. From the mud on the boots of the tall one I perceive that he comes from South Norwood. The other is obviously a Scotch author.'

'How can you tell that?'

'He is carrying in his pocket a book called (I clearly see) Auld Licht Something.

Would anyone but the author be likely to carry about a book with such a title?'

I had to confess that this was improbable.

It was now evident that the two men (if such they can be called) were seeking our lodgings. I have said (often) that my friend Holmes seldom gave way to emotion of any kind, but now he turned livid with passion. Presently this gave place to a strange look of triumph.

'Watson,' he said, 'that big fellow has for years taken the credit for my most remarkable doings, but at last I have him – at last!'

Up I went to the ceiling and when I returned the strangers were in the room.

'I perceive, gentlemen', said Mr Sherlock Holmes, 'that you are at present afflicted by an extraordinary novelty.'

The handsomer of our visitors asked in amazement how he knew this, but the big one only scowled.

'You forget that you wear a ring on your fourth finger', replied Mr Holmes calmly.

I was about to jump to the ceiling when the big brute interposed.

'That Tommy-rot is all very well for the public, Holmes', said he, 'but you can drop it for me. And, Watson, if you go up to the ceiling again I shall make you stay there.'

Here I observed a curious phenomenon. My friend Sherlock Holmes *shrank*. He became small before my eyes. I looked longingly at the ceiling, but dared not.

'Let us cut the first four pages', said the big man, 'and proceed to business. I want to know why . . .'

'Allow me', said Mr Holmes with some of his old courage. 'You want to know why the public does not go to your opera.'

'Exactly', said the other, ironically, 'as you perceive by my shirt stud.' He added more gravely: 'And as you can only find out in one way I must insist on your witnessing an entire performance of the piece.'

It was an anxious moment for me, I shuddered, for I knew that if Holmes went, I should have to go with him. But my friend had a heart of gold. 'Never', he cried, fiercely. 'I will do anything for you save that.'

'Your continued existence depends on it', said the big man, menacingly.

'I would rather melt into air', replied Holmes, proudly taking another chair. 'But I can tell you why the public don't go to your piece without sitting the thing out myself.'

'Why?'

'Because', replied Holmes calmly, 'they prefer to stay away.'

A dead silence followed that extraordinary remark. For a moment the two intruders gazed with awe upon the man who had unravelled their mystery so wonderfully. Then drawing their knives . . .

Holmes grew less and less, until nothing was left save a ring of smoke which slowly circled to the ceiling.

The last words of great men are often noteworthy. These were the last words of Sherlock Holmes; 'Fool, fool! I have kept you in luxury for years. By my help you have ridden extensively in cabs, where no author was ever seen before. *Henceforth you will ride in buses!*'

The brute sank into a chair aghast. The other author did not turn a hair.

To A. Conan Doyle,
From his friend,
J. M. Barrie


Curiously, the success of the plays lay to some extent in the Holmes character's resemblance to Sidney Paget's drawings, which leaned more towards his brother than Conan Doyle's original description.

Conan Doyle and his wife, Louise, on a two-seater tricycle outside their South
Norwood home. From an article titled *A Day with Dr Conan Doyle* written by Harry
How, which appeared in *Strand* magazine in 1892.

'All the impersonations of Holmes and all the drawings are very unlike my own idea of the man', Doyle once commented. 'I saw him as very tall – "over six feet but so excessively lean that he seemed considerably taller", said *A Study in Scarlet*. He had, as I imagined him, a thin, razor-like face with a great hawk's bill of a nose, and two small eyes set close together on either side of it.' Doyle, however, enjoyed the primitive Sherlock Holmes films which appeared before his death, despite their liberal use of fast cars and telephones, which did not widely exist in Holmes's day.

Conan Doyle devoted himself very seriously to the business of writing. There was no mystical process, waiting on the chance visit of inspiration. Writing was a job, a living to be earned, and he applied himself industriously to the task from breakfast to lunch and from five o'clock until eight in the evening.

In the afternoons ideas came to him as he walked, played cricket and tennis or pedalled his lumbering two-seater tricycle around the quiet lanes of South Norwood. At his desk, working on a new Holmes story, his first task would be to conjure the ending. Then he carefully constructed a trail winding up to it, concealing the solution until the latest possible moment. When he felt that the mix was right, Conan Doyle would often bet his wife Louise a shillling that she could not guess the outcome. Such was his pursuit of craftsmanship and perfection that one of his reasons for delaying Holmes's return was that he was 'fearful of spoiling' the character.

On the day intrepid reporter Harry How visited Doyle to write a *Strand* profile. The author was sorting through a typical mail delivery. 'On the morning of my visit the particulars of a poisoning case had been sent to him from New Zealand, and the previous day a great packet of documents relating to a disputed will had been received from Bristol. Other letters come from people reading his stories, saying whether they guessed the mystery or not . . .' It was this aspect of critical admiration from his readers which made the author constantly sharpen both the mysteries and Holmes's powers of observation. But inevitably for a man whose own skills were not highly developed in this direction, irregularities crept into the adventures.

'Sometimes I have got upon dangerous ground where I have taken risks through my own want of knowledge of the correct atmosphere', Conan Doyle wrote in his memoirs. 'I have, for example, never been a racing man, and yet I ventured to write *The Silver Blaze* in which the mystery depends on the laws of training and racing.

'The story is all right, and Holmes may have been at the top of his form, but my ignorance cries aloud to heaven. I read an excellent and very damaging criticism of the story in some sporting paper, written clearly by a man who *did* know, in which he explained the exact penalties which would have come upon everyone concerned if they had acted as I described. Half would have been in jail and the other half warned off the Turf forever. However, I have never been nervous about details, and one must be masterful sometimes. When an alarmed editor wrote to me once: "There is no second line of rails at this point", I answered: "I make one."'

His bravado extended beyond the Holmes stories. In 1912, Greenhough Smith, reading the manuscript of *The Lost World*, tentatively pointed out that a balloon made from stitched animal hides would have been too heavy to lift itself from the ground. 'The gas', came Doyle's lightning reply, 'was Lovogen, a volcanic product peculiar to plateau conditions, which has been calculated by Prof. T. E. S. Tube, FRS, to be 35,371 times lighter than hydrogen.' The editor was greatly amused, but wisely did not press the point further.

While Doyle was happy to admit his shortcomings and reply to hair-splitting questions with tongue firmly in cheek, such a relaxed outlook has eluded the body of Holmesian scholarship. Incongruities are a source of great concern, and various despairing efforts have been made to explain them away. None, perhaps, quite so extreme as the mathematics lecturer from

Sherlock Holmes in *The Silver Blaze.*

the University of Georgia who postulated that the errors were intentional. 'Conan Doyle was creating a character with keen and accurate powers of observation, who decried the lack of observation in others', Pope R. Hill deduced. 'To prove his point that people do not observe, he put in simple and obvious errors wholesale... Conan Doyle tried to fool the world and he succeeded beyond his wildest dreams.' Except, of course, for the hawk-eyed Mr Pope R. Hill.

The slightest references have sent flurries of anxiety through the Holmesian community. Watson, planning to share rooms with the detective in *A Study in Scarlet* remarks, 'I keep a bull pup'; but the spectral dog never appears through sixty stories to sully the bear-skin rug of 221B. Holmesians eagerly seized on a suggestion that 'to keep a bull pup' was Anglo-Indian cant meaning to have a temper, but it does not appear in any of the standard dictionaries of historical slang.

Arguments have raged over apparent mathematical inconsistencies, from the method Holmes used to calculate the train's speed of 53.5 mph by counting telegraph poles, in *The Silver Blaze*, to the twenty-degree inaccuracy of a seventeenth-century compass in *The Musgrave Ritual*. Even the normally-obtuse Watson noticed his friend's peaks and troughs: 'Now and again, however, it chanced that even when he erred the truth was still discovered. I have notes of some half-dozen cases of the kind', he observed in *The Yellow Face*.

Mrs Hudson, the landlady whose 'stately tread' was a comforting feature of life in Baker Street, is a source of further consternation. The lady who brings in the tray in *A Scandal in Bohemia* is – lo and behold – a complete stranger named Mrs Turner, never referred to elsewhere in the stories. Is she Mrs Hudson's sister? The relative of some previous marriage to a Mr Turner? The housekeeper from one of Holmes's strange 'accommodation addresses'? A friend helping out? A temporary maid? Or perhaps Conan Doyle may have occasionally had a human lapse of memory.

Much of the 'higher criticism' of Sherlock Holmes, one would like to believe, is written in fun; a mischievous parody of classical scholarship. But, alas, the jape has extended to those unfamiliar with the rules. Pages have been devoted to the quality of Holmes's violin varnish, and a whole volume (*The Man Who Seldom Laughed*) to his '316 responses to humorous situations or statements', including 103 smiles, 65 laughs, 58 jokes, 31 chuckles and 59 other variations. There are, says D. A. N. Jones, two forms of the Sherlock Holmes game. 'One is: Let's pretend Sherlock Holmes was real, an eminent Victorian with a complicated life for biographers to unravel. The other is: Let's pretend Conan Doyle was a great writer like Sophocles or Shakespeare, whose text deserves structured analysis...' The truth is that Doyle was a highly skilled story-teller, one of the finest of his calling – a point grasped by the general reader who enjoys Holmes as much as his great-grandfather who queued for the *Strand*, but sadly lost by a handful of devotees afflicted with tunnel vision.

The great detective has been put under the magnifying glass for almost a century since he first appeared in print. There is probably little of the amiable, gregarious Conan Doyle in him. 'If I have sometimes been inclined to weary of him', he said, 'it is because his character admits no light or shade. He is a calculating machine...' If we wish to seek the author anywhere he is more likely to be found in Watson. Not necessarily in the fellow doctor, the writer or the 'severely practical' character who 'always keeps us flat-footed on the ground'. In the light of the brilliant detective Doyle and Watson were pleasingly ordinary. 'Watson', remarked Doyle before his death, 'was not really stupid at all. He was simply just the average man.' Harry How walked up the writer's garden path to find that 'there was nothing lynx-eyed, nothing "detective" about him – not even the regulation walk of our modern solver of mysteries. He is just a happy, genial, homely man; tall, broad-shouldered, with a hand that grips you heartily and, in its sincerity of welcome, hurts.'

The adventures of Holmes and Watson, for all their entertaining complexity, sophisticated deduction and intriguing detail, are escapism in its finest form. Conan Doyle would probably have been perplexed if more had been attributed to them than was necessary. In announcing the final appearance of the ageing detective in 1927 he wrote: 'And so, reader, Farewell to Sherlock Holmes. I thank you for your constancy, and can but hope that some return has been made in the shape of that distraction from the worries of life and stimulating change of thought which can only be found in the fairy kingdom of romance.'

# PART II
# A Case of Identity

Sherlock Holmes: the world's first consulting detective.

# On the Trail of the World's First Consulting Detective

EIGHTEEN HUNDRED and fifty four was a very good year for Holmes readers. So, too, were 1852, 1853 and 1855; while others prefer 1857, 1858 and 1867 – all years in which students of the great investigator have pinpointed his birth. The precise location is another problem. Yorkshire's North Riding is the unanimous favourite, but some claim that he originates from Surrey (a theory prompted by his passing interest in newspaper county cricket scores), though Holmes seems far too outspoken for a Home Counties man. With Yorkshire's reputation for claiming that all national superlatives emanate from its boundaries, it is perhaps inevitable that even Sherlock Holmes should be a Tyke.

There have been many determined efforts to establish his genealogy and early life, most of them a heady mix of inspired juxtaposition, clever assumption and guesswork. Like all the better Holmesian research, it is artfully provocative stuff. Heraldry enthusiasts have suggested coats of arms and family mottoes. Of these the timorous 'We Can But Try', proposed by American Rolfe Boswell, seems hardly appropriate for the assertive Holmes; Belden Wigglesworth's 'I Think, Therefore I Am' a little too abstract for a man of action. 'Just And Firm Of Purpose', researched by William S. Hall (argent, three buglehorns, sable with lion rampant) is perhaps more what we would expect from as rare a creature as a sophisticated Yorkshireman.

Theories tumble with wit and erudition, arrogance and wild assumption, in attempts to clothe the world's most famous detective with greater reality than even Conan Doyle could muster.

His mother's Christian name has been suggested as Violet, because it 'belonged to three ladies whom Holmes treated with more than ordinary courtesy'. The manufactured minutiae of his private life are endless. Holmes's handwriting has been analysed by an eminent graphologist, his horoscope cast in *Prediction* magazine, and his birthday claimed as 6th January (on the basis that *Twelfth Night* is the only play he quotes from twice). There is still controversy about whether his birth-stone is emerald or garnet. Years of research have poured into gleaning such fragments. The stratosphere of Holmesian studies includes *How Holmes Came to Play the Violin*, by Prof. Jacques Barzum, Sherlock Holmes's *Wanderjahre* by A. Carson Simpson, even *Was Sherlock Holmes an American?* by the distinguished Christopher Morley. The general reader is on safer ground studying Holmes and Watson from the Authorised Version of the original Conan Doyle stories, which piece together an intriguing picture of the world's first consulting detective and his right-hand man.

## Pipe-smoking Bachelor Detective Seeks Flatmate

HOLMES AS A YOUNG man was a reclusive individual. During two years at college, he tells Watson in *The Gloria Scott*, he made only one friend, Victor Trevor.

'I was never a very sociable fellow, always rather fond of moping in my rooms and working out my own little methods of thought, so that I never mixed much with the men of my year.'

He was too preoccupied to be lonely, and took part in boxing and fencing, but was in need of understanding friends. Throughout his life Holmes rarely made time for small talk or cultivated acquaintances. He developed a long list of contacts for work, but his private circle remained small.

His sparse social life at college can be blamed partly on his course, which is never specifically mentioned in the stories: 'My line of study was quite distinct from that of the other fellows, so that we had no points of contact at all.' Girls and hard drinking, the currency of student life, were absent from his somewhat austere existence. Trevor, 'A hearty, full-blooded fellow, full of spirit and energy', was quite the opposite of the brooding, lethargic Holmes. They met the day Trevor's bull-terrier seized Holmes by the ankle as he walked to chapel, and laid him up for ten days. Holmes, withdrawn and diffident, was slow to make friends, but Trevor's visits to his sick-bed lengthened until they became quite close. How close no one has had the impropriety to inquire, but their relationship quickly became 'a bond of union' when Trevor confessed that he also was without chums, which seems curious for such a hearty, full-blooded fellow. They appeared to get along well together as, by the end of term, Holmes was invited to the family home at Donnithorpe, Norfolk, for a month in the long vacation.

Holmes grew up to acquire an easy manner with all kinds of people within the sharply divided compartments of the Victorian class system. He had an engaging informality with street urchins and royalty alike, but it was a façade acquired from habit. Beneath it Holmes found socializing irksome. 'This', he said, fingering a crested, monogrammed envelope in *The Noble Bachelor*, 'looks like one of those unwelcome social summonses which call upon a man either to be bored or to lie.'

Inevitably, constant exposure to human weakness and the grimy side of life began to affect him, clouding his outlook but stopping short of obscuring his judgment. The burden of being the unsung arbiter of justice was to lose any enjoyment for the simplicities of life. Where others saw beauty, Holmes saw vulnerability. The spectre of crime hung everywhere, like the exorcist who sees evil where none yet exists.

'Do you know, Watson', he says rather bleakly in *The Copper Beeches*, 'it is one of the curses of a mind with a turn like mine that I must look at everything with reference to my own special subject. You look at these scattered houses, and you are impressed by their beauty. I look at them and the only thought which comes to me is a feeling of their isolation, and of the impunity with which crime may be committed there.' Lesser men, unable to separate their line of work from relaxation, have suffered mental breakdowns, but Holmes was made of stronger stuff.

The pressure of constantly outwitting greed and criminal ingenuity might build up until he felt inclined to seize a ruffian by the lapels, but normally he disguised his emotions well. When his anger did boil to the surface there were undertones of violence. Holmes flushed with fury at the thought of James Windibank escaping justice in *A Case of Identity*: 'By Jove! It is not part of my duties to my client, but here's a hunting-crop handy, and I think I shall just treat myself to...' The unpleasant Mr Windibank wisely took to his heels. In different circumstances he could turn his

Holmes sees off the 'unpleasant Mr Windibank' in *A Case of Identity*.

feelings to the cutting sleight. Even the King of Bohemia was not above the Holmes cold shoulder. 'He bowed and turning away without observing the hand which the King had stretched out to him, he set off in my company to his chambers', Watson recorded.

Holmes's bizarre life left no room for romance. The Work was his mistress, dictating his moods and inspiration; without it he sank into boredom and the refuge of cocaine. Casework was his real drug, transporting him in bursts of energy to intellectual euphoria. When the great mind was at full stretch everything and everyone – including those who came to him for help – became secondary. 'The status of my client is a matter of less moment to me than the interest of his case', he firmly declared in *The Noble Bachelor*.

In *The Greek Interpreter* Watson perceives Holmes as 'a brain without a heart, as deficient in human sympathy as he was pre-eminent in intelligence'.

A life which plots a graph of such extremes, 'admitting neither light nor shade' as Conan Doyle put it, creates a dual nature. Holmes swung from high excitement to deep melancholy, leaving poor Watson to cope with his wild pendulum. Some see it as the expression of a superior man, whose motivation was to rise above the mundane by taking on challenges which stretched him to his limits. 'There is nothing more stimulating than a case where everything goes against you', he says under pressure in *The Hound of the Baskervilles*. Others, like Christopher Isherwood, saw Holmes as the ultimate amateur detective, 'one of the truly great comic characters in our literature'. Admittedly his behaviour veers towards the absurd at times, but Doyle always managed to keep a rein on his credibility.

Holmes's rural beginnings moulded him less than the tough realities of urban life. Like dozens of later fictional heroes he was the quintessential city detective, at home in dim dockland alleys or the palatial splendour of Belgravia. Despite being the first in a profession preoccupied with earning a living, money was of little consideration. Hunger for knowledge – whether bent over test tubes seeking new directions in forensic science, or scrutinizing people – drove him along. Yet, in his fascination with the small points of appearance, the details of gesture and speech, he missed the richness of relationships. The art of deduction reduced everyone he met to the level of a litmus held up to the light. Watson, in one of his rare flashes of perception, saw his friend, in *The Greek Interpreter*, as 'a brain without a heart, as deficient in human sympathy as he was pre-eminent in intelligence', which was also Doyle's view entirely.

Holmes was an emotional defective by choice, not circumstance. It would be tempting to feel sympathetic with a man whose pursuit of high ideals somehow left him sadly lacking, if it were not for the fact that he systematically suppressed and excluded all traces of emotion. 'The emotional qualities are antagonistic to clear reasoning', he stated with cold conviction in *The Sign of Four*. His reverence for reason and pursuit of logic made him a difficult companion – secretive, moody and with a humour which bordered on false heartiness. Perhaps only the well-adjusted and long-suffering Watson could have put up with him.

He was not without sensitivity, coaxing melancholy chords from his Stradivarius or relaxing with his rare books. This, perhaps, was a glimpse of the real Holmes, the human face which emerged only behind the closed doors of Baker Street, On one occasion the feelings he struggled hard to sublimate surfaced in public, to the amazement of onlookers. Lost in thought in *The Naval Treaty*, he holds up a rose and tells those around him: 'Our highest assurance of the goodness of Providence seems to me to rest in the flowers. All other things, our powers, our desires, our food are really necessary for our existence in the first instance. But this rose is an extra ... It is only goodness which gives extras ...' Whether Conan Doyle wrote this with a hint of a smile, we shall never know.

Holmes, transported by a rose, betrays a rare glimpse of sensitivity in *The Naval Treaty*.

## Sex and the Single Investigator

WOMEN WOULD CERTAINLY have found prolonged exposure to the great detective insufferable. As an investigator he had a healthy respect for their intuition, but he remained uncomfortable and reserved when dealing with them. Holmes was out of his element with the opposite sex. Intellectual achievement was clearly no help in such matters; spontaneity and emotional depth left him much to puzzle over. 'Their most trivial action may mean volumes, or their most extraordinary conduct may depend upon a hair-pin or curling-tongs', he pondered in *The Second Stain*.

He has all the appearance of a misogynist, but it is kinder to suppose that he was one of that rare and all-but-extinct breed, The Great British Bachelor. Holmes the consulting detective could turn on the professional charm to reassure a distressed client. Miss Stoner confesses her terror to him in *The Speckled Band*, raising her veil to reveal 'a state of pitiable agitation'.

' "You must not fear", said he soothingly, bending forward and patting her forearm. "We shall soon set matters right, I have no doubt." '

As the accomplished actor and master of disguise he could slip into any part, even that of the seducer, with ease. In the case of *Charles Augustus Milverton*, 'the worst man in all London', Holmes dressed as a self-employed plumber in order to obtain information from Milverton's housemaid. Safely back in Baker Street he removed his disguise, sat by the fire and 'laughed heartily in his silent, inward fashion', perhaps as much in surprise at his conquest as at the success of his ruse. Milverton was undoubtedly a bad egg and an unmitigated bounder, but Holmes carried his role

beyond professional requirements and, astonishingly, proposed to her.

'Surely you have gone too far,' cries Watson in alarm.

'It was a most necessary step,' Holmes claims, barely able to conceal his pleasure. 'I have walked out with her each evening, and I have talked with her. Good heavens, those talks! However, I have got all I wanted . . .'

Holmes was, of course, referring solely to evidence gleaned in the course of duty, but the encounter certainly perked his sometimes jaded sprits.

He was aware of the strength of his passions. In *The Devil's Foot* he confesses that he has never been in love. But if he had, he says, and the woman he loved had been poisoned like the victim of the story, he would have gone to any length to seek revenge.

On rare occasions, in the presence of a striking woman, Holmes appears to have difficulty controlling his troublesome juices. In *The Solitary Cyclist* he found it impossible to refuse the 'young and beautiful woman, tall and queenly', who rapped on the front door of Baker Street one night to beg his assistance. Despite the late hour his irritable nature melted. He seemed to struggle to resist her obvious charm.

Holmes asked her what was troubling her: ' "At least it cannot be your health," said he, as his keen eyes darted over her; "so ardent a cyclist must be full of energy." '

He then 'took the lady's ungloved hand and examined it with as close an attention and as little sentiment as a scientist would show to a specimen'.

'You will excuse me, I am sure. It is my business,' he murmurs.

A moment later he was touching her cheek: ' "There is a spirituality about the face" – he gently turned it towards the

Holmes's low regard for women led to his being outwitted by Irene Adler in *A Scandal in Bohemia*. The beautiful contralto not only saw through his disguise, but followed him undetected, disguised as 'a slim youth in an Ulster'.

light . . .' Given the formality of the times it was certainly curious professional behaviour for a gentleman with a lady client in the privacy of his rooms late at night, whatever her distress.

On other occasions, relaxing with the good Watson, his only confidante, he let slip his inhibitions about the opposite sex. Holmes felt that he could never trust a woman for fear that any close relationship would erode his powers of perception. They were his most precious possession, which not even love could be allowed to intrude upon. The prospect of losing his head over a woman was perhaps his greatest fear. When

Watson tells him, at the end of *The Sign of Four*, that he is to marry Mary Morstan, Holmes's tactless reaction is to emit 'a most dismal groan'. His fixed views on the subject prevent him even from wishing his only friend well.

'I really cannot congratulate you', he says disapprovingly.

Watson, understandably, is a little hurt and to smooth things Holmes clumsily adds: 'I think she is one of the most charming young ladies I ever met, and might have been most useful in such work as we have been doing.'

He cannot resist using the occasion to

express his own restricted opinion: 'Love is an emotional thing', he tells the ever-patient Watson, 'and whatever is emotional is opposed to that true, cold reason which I place above all things. I should never marry myself, lest I bias my judgement.'

With the case successfully concluded, and Watson happily engaged, what is left for the great mind to occupy itself? ' "For me," said Sherlock Holmes, "there still remains the cocaine-bottle." And he stretched his long, white hand up for it.'

From this it would seem that Holmes's despair arises from his own innate selfishness, but, as always, there was perhaps more to the master than he cared to admit. Little more than a year previously he had been badly shaken by the unthinkable, seemingly impossible occasion of being outwitted by a woman. More precisely, *the* woman, as Watson called her in *A Scandal in Bohemia*. The dazzlingly beautiful contralto, Irene Adler – adored at La Scala and the Imperial Opera of Warsaw alike – shook his confidence so badly that he kept a photograph of her to remind himself that it could never be allowed to happen again. Irene out-manoeuvred him, forecast his moves and saw through his disguise. She even followed him herself, undetected, disguised as 'a slim youth in an Ulster' and bade him goodnight. No mean feat considering Watson's recollection of her 'superb figure'.

Her cunning triumphed because of

Holmes meets Miss Violet Hunter in *The Copper Beeches*. Watson's hopes for a romantic attachment between the two sadly came to nothing.

Holmes's blind spot, allowing his low regard for women to cloud his judgment. While he has been accused of overestimating the abilities of his male adversaries, he made the fundamental error of underestimating women. Had he Watson's appreciative eye for a pretty face, the embarrassing debacle might not have occurred.

'What a very attractive woman!' Watson exclaims, first setting eyes on Mary Morstan.

'Is she?' Holmes remarks languidly, 'I did not observe.'

'You really are an automation – a calculating machine', Watson says in exasperation. 'There is something positively inhuman in you at times.'

It was a trait the normally-meticulous Holmes should have come to grips with but, because of the nature of the subject, he considered it of little importance.

In *The Copper Beeches* his professional manner is at its patronizing best as he sits with his client, Miss Violet Hunter:

'I should feel so much stronger if I felt that you were at the back of me', she flutters.

'Oh, you may carry that feeling away with you', Holmes replies, stopping short of patting her. 'I assure you that your little problem promises to be the most interesting which has come my way for some months.'

The encounter raised Watson's romantic hopes for his friend. Alas, he was forced to record that Holmes, 'rather to my disappointment, manifested no further interest in her when once she had ceased to be the centre of one of his problems, and she is now the head of a private school at Walsall, where I believe that she has met with considerable success'.

Despite what appears to be disturbing evidence to the contrary, Sherlock Holmes could not have been without a glimmer of unfulfilled desire. So what, if anything, was his image of the perfect woman? The opposite sex, by definition, was incapable of perfection; but if we conclude that he might be attracted to anyone who mirrored his own attributes, then Irene Adler came close. In Holmes's view it would, of course, be impossible for mere womankind to equal him intellectually; an outlook further complicated by Victorian social attitudes, which did not expect female talent to extend beyond the embroidery frame. The role of middle class women was firmly confined to raising children, organizing household staff and paying social calls; a notion which coloured the attitude of most professional men of the period. However, thanks to the example of a handful of single-minded females who battled with the prejudices of the era, a New Woman was quietly emerging – spirited, bright and independent. Holmes, like many of his well-to-do brothers, was quite unprepared for this. At the best of times he found that 'woman's heart and mind are insoluble problems to the male'. The new breed of self-assured women was beyond his cloistered experience of close encounters with the opposite sex.

An outstanding Society beauty with a 'dark, handsome clear-cut face', unexpectedly pulls a small revolver on the dastardly Charles Augustus Milverton. Holmes, known for his lightning reactions, does nothing to stop her as she squeezes the trigger, shouting 'Take that you hound, and that! – and that! – and that!' The ever-ready Watson leaps to wrestle the gun from her, but is held back: 'I felt Holmes' cold, strong grasp upon my wrist. I understood the whole argument of that firm, restraining grip – that it was no affair of ours.' Holmes's idea of justice appears satisfied when she grinds her heel into Milverton's upturned

Holmes is confronted by the forceful Mrs Neville St Clair in *The Man with the Twisted Lip.*

face. Remarkably, he then bolts the door at the sound of footsteps to allow her to escape. Later, impressed by the way in which she planned the episode and entered the house in disguise, he drags Watson to an Oxford Street photographer's shop to point out excitedly the singular lady's portrait. 'My eyes met those of Holmes, and he put his finger to his lips as we turned away from the window.'

Holmes may have had a sneaking admiration for such fearlessly independent females, but he was also nervous of them. Perhaps it was their abrasiveness which disturbed his equilibrium. When he had to report to Mrs Neville St Clair about her missing husband, in *The Man with the Twisted Lip*, he wisely enlisted Watson's support ('You'll come with me, won't you?'). Before they had even time to knock, 'the door flew open and a little blonde

woman stood in the opening, clad in some sort of light *mousseline-de-soie*, with a touch of fluffy pink chiffon at her neck and wrists'. Hardly the demure, wilting type upon whom Holmes would normally exude his professional charm.

'Well?' she demanded, 'Well?' – to which the speechless Holmes could do nothing but helplessly shrug his shoulders. Her response was to let out a groan. Mrs St Clair led them to the dining-room and immediately buckled down to business: 'I should very much like to ask you one or two plain questions, to which I beg that you will give me a plain answer ... Do not trouble about my feelings. I am not hysterical or given to fainting.'

Mrs St Clair asked about her husband. 'Sherlock Holmes seemed to be embarrassed by the question. "Frankly now!" she repeated, standing upon the rug, and looking keenly down at him, as he leaned back in a basket chair . . .'

Holmes embarrassed was a curious phenomenon. His concern about taking the stalwart Watson along for company became clearer when it was revealed that the attractive, intimidating Mrs St Clair had invited him to stay the night in 'a large and comfortable double-bedded room'. The untroubled Watson slept soundly, waking at dawn to find that Holmes had been sitting bolt upright all night smoking shag tobacco. We can only assume from this that his full attention had been devoted to the problems of a difficult case. Had he been alone, the superb analytical mind might have been distracted by greater worries.

## The Seven Per Cent Solution

IT WAS SMALL WONDER that Sherlock Holmes was prone to moods of deep emptiness. He had a few sporting activities and hobbies to balance his dedication to the Method, but they were always linked in some way to work. Without the demands of a case to solve, and his self-imposed abstinence from female companionship, there was only the dubious solace of drugs.

Holmes became attracted by the effects of cocaine three years after Josef Brettauer, a Trieste surgeon, demonstrated its use as an anaesthetic at the Heidelberg Congress of Ophthalmology in 1884. Its painkilling properties had been discovered by Karl Koller while working alongside Freud at Vienna's Allgemeines Krankenhaus on cures for morphine addiction.

Conan Doyle, as an eye specialist himself, would have been familiar with Brettauer's historic operation. Cocaine was hailed as a wonder drug, but, though it was not officially recognized as addictive until after

World War I, Watson became suspicious of his friend's dependence on it. Holmes was injecting himself three times a day with a 7 per cent solution; an amount lower than the 10 per cent standard medical dosage of the period, but a sufficiently high daily intake to cause concern. His rooms, which had always had an untidy, Bohemian air, were becoming the dishevelled quarters of the *habitué*. In *The Dying Detective*, Watson describes the mantelpiece as 'a litter of pipes, tobacco pouches, syringes, penknives, revolver cartridges and other debris'.

Holmes's depression and fluctuating moods may well have been intensified by cocaine, rather than alleviated by it. But

Holmes found solace in drugs.

the detective, laden with ennui, believed that its effect outweighed the risks to his health.

'I suppose that its influence is physically a bad one', he admits in *The Sign of Four*. 'I find it, however, so transcendently stimulating and clarifying to the mind that its secondary action is a matter of small moment.' Pessimism was probably an occupational hazard, but a man given to philosophizing on the futility of life is least suited to finding relief from drugs. 'We reach. We grasp', he says in *The Retired Colourman*. 'And what is left at the end? A shadow. Or worse than a shadow – misery.'

The bachelor who distrusted women because they might interfere with his reasoning had little resistance to a substance which could destroy the same powers chemically. Watson's sound arguments did little to sway him:

'But consider!' he pleads. 'Count the cost! Your brain may, as you say, be roused and excited, but it is a pathological and morbid process, which involves increased tissue change and may at last leave a permanent weakness. You know, too, what a blank reaction comes upon you. Surely the game

is hardly worth a candle. Why should you, for a mere passing pleasure, risk the loss of those great powers with which you have been endowed? Remember that I speak not only as one comrade to another, but as a medical man to one for whose constitution he is to some extent answerable.'

As a medical man in general practice Watson had a knowledge of the effects of cocaine which, in his day, would perhaps have exceeded that of a family doctor. As a friend to Holmes, he probably read up its properties in medical journals. Doyle himself, according to Prof. Michael Shepherd of the Institute of Psychiatry, took the drug gelsemium in experiments which he reported to the *British Medical Journal* in 1879. His studies may have given him the idea of adding the dimension of Holmes's addiction to the stories.

The detective knew that his own cure lay in work, but sufficiently taxing cases were not always available to occupy him. 'Give me problems, give me work, give me the most abstruse cryptogram, or the most intricate analysis, and I am in my own proper atmosphere. I can dispense then with artificial stimulants.' Despite Holmes's heavy

Holmes injected himself three times a day with a 7 per cent solution of cocaine.

use of cocaine, Watson was reluctant to broach the subject because his friend managed to effect such a 'cool, nonchalant air'. Yet the sight of his companion injecting himself in the privacy of 221B made him extremely irritable. For months Watson watched in despair as Holmes prepared his solution three times daily and, on one occasion, even offered him a 'fix':

'Sherlock Holmes took his bottle from the corner of the mantelpiece, and his hypodermic syringe from its neat morocco case. With his long, white, nervous fingers he adjusted the delicate needle, and rolled back his left shirt-cuff. For some little time his eyes rested thoughtfully upon the sinewy forearm and wrist, all dotted and scarred with innumerable puncture marks. Finally, he thrust the sharp point home, pressed down the tiny piston, and sank back into the velvet-lined armchair with a long sigh of satisfaction.'

Inevitably, a Holmesian scholar of the Ubermensch school has neatly come to terms with the notion of the master being a junkie by postulating that it was all an elaborate practical joke on poor Watson. Dr George F. McCleary suggests that readers should 'assume that he did not actually take the drug, but mystified Watson into believing that he did'. The trick in writing about Holmes is that, as long as the tone is sombre and studious enough, the most elastic theories can be given weighty consideration. 'The rule of the game', said the late crime-writer, Dorothy M. Sayers, 'is that it must be played as solemnly as a county cricket match at Lord's; the slightest touch of extravagance or burlesque ruins the atmosphere.' Miss Sayers was the author of the penetrating *Dr Watson's Christian Name*.

Eventually Holmes, with the help of his good friend, appears to have reduced his cocaine habit to a containable level. The detective reciprocated with patient understanding about the doctor's gambling habits.

## The Mystery of the Missing House

WHEN THE BRICKLAYERS, carpenters and stonemasons of late eighteenth-century London rumbled into Marylebone on wagons groaning with building materials they had little idea they would be constructing one of the best-loved streets in British fiction. The Portman family, who owned the valuable parcel of land, envisaged a prestigious quarter-mile thoroughfare running towards the heart of the West End. The flat-fronted Georgian town houses, rising three storeys with servants' accommodation squeezed beneath the roof, were interspersed with fashionable shops and studios. The Portmans named the street in honour of a family friend and neighbour, Sir Edward Baker, a Dorset landowner. When he died in 1825 his name passed into obscurity, but the fame of Baker Street spread around the world when Sherlock Holmes moved from lodgings in Montague Street, Bloomsbury, and took rooms at 221B.

The exact location of the fictitious number remained Conan Doyle's secret. An 1876 street map shows houses numbered only up to 84, the street ending abruptly in a northerly direction at Paddington Street. Buildings were renumbered long ago, and some pulled down, leaving a critical gap between 219 and 225, which was eventually filled by the headquarters of the Abbey National Building Society. The bricks of the demolished house were preserved by the company and sold as souvenirs. Today the Holmes connection is perpetuated by a secretary on the fourth floor who replies to letters which still arrive at the rate of fifty a week, addressed to S. Holmes, Esq.

The curious trickle of correspondence – from little boys soliciting help to find lost marbles, to wealthy Americans anxious to hire his services – began by accident in 1937. A postman wondering where to deliver a letter from two Danish pensioners asking Holmes's advice on how to buy a shop for their retirement, found himself outside Abbey House. By some mysterious process of reasoning he glanced at the name-plates and decided to leave it at the offices of the British Home Stores, on the third floor. The fact that the elderly Danish couple never benefitted from the great man's services has done little to deter thousands of other correspondents.

Doyle made it clear in the stories that Holmes and Watson lived in Baker Street, Marylebone (though there is a well-argued theory that it may have been Baker Street, Brixton, with which he was equally familiar), and the most valuable clue to the precise location of 221B is found in *The Empty House*. It was set at the time the two friends were reunited after the Reichenbach Falls incident, and were back at work again 'in the dark jungle of criminal London'. Holmes placed a wax bust of himself in the window of their rooms to lure Col. Sebastian Moran into shooting him. They took a cab to Baker Street to lie in wait, but paid off the driver in Cavendish Square.

Holmes then led his friend on foot through a maze of mews and stables into Blandford Street, which runs westward to meet Baker Street at right angles. Before they reached the junction Holmes ducked into a narrow passage – whether it was to the right or left of Blandford Street, we do not know – and opened a wooden gate which led into a deserted yard at the back of an empty house on Baker Street. From one of the rooms they could see directly across to their own accommodation. 'We are in Camden House', Holmes whispers, 'which stands opposite to our own old quarters.'

Mercifully for the real-life residents of Baker Street, Camden House was a figment of Doyle's imagination. Years of surveys and amateur detective work have left enthusiasts still in conflict about the exact address. A further clue, often used as a cross reference, is the mystery of the missing lamp-post. Watson records that the front room of their vantage point, the empty house, was 'faintly lit in the centre from the lights of the street beyond'. But there was, he adds, 'no lamp near'. Indefatigable Holmesians who have unearthed contemporary street maps find that lamp-posts are clearly marked on them. Houses between street lights near the Blandford Street junction narrow the field considerably. Of these, Harold Atkins in the *Daily Telegraph* in 1960 pinpointed what was No. 61 in Doyle's day as the empty house. Years later it was renumbered 51, then demolished to make way for the extension of Druce's store. Finally, most of the site was flattened in the Blitz, so Doyle's tracks have been well covered by the march of history.

If we had crossed the granite sets of Baker Street from the empty house in Holmes's day, and opened the front door, we would probably have been given a quizzical look by Mr Peterson, the commissionaire. He was employed by a company renting the ground floor offices, and left the glowing fire in his recess to monitor comings and goings. The basement kitchen was the domain of Mrs Hudson, the landlady who 'did' for them: took up visiting cards from callers, and cast withering looks at the Baker Street Irregulars, the band of ragamuffins who ran errands for the detective. Holmes and Watson's accommodation was on the first

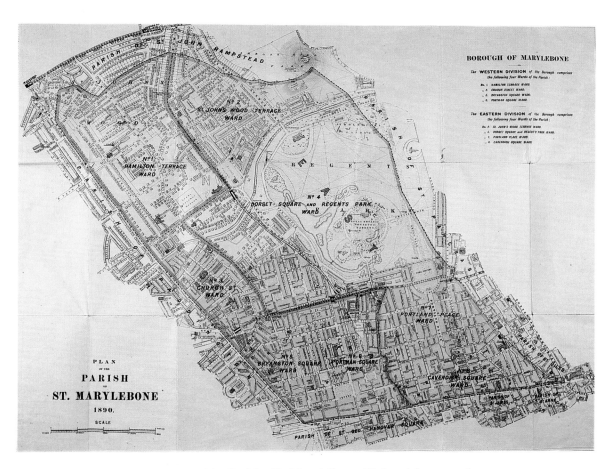

An 1890 map of the Parish of St Marylebone – Holmes's home territory.

The City of London area where Conan Doyle's publishers, *Strand* magazine, had their offices.

floor, 'a couple of comfortable bedrooms, and a single airy sitting-room, cheerfully furnished and illuminated by two broad windows'.

The shared sitting-room would have had the velvet drapes, durable carpets, heavy wallpaper and claustrophobic comfort of the era, coupled with the general untidiness of a typical bachelor apartment. There were gas-lamps with glowing yellow mantles on the wall and a fire-place by which Holmes brooded on long winter evenings. Gas had been piped to Baker Street for some years; its popularity increased when the South Metropolitan Gas Company installed a hundred slot meters in London homes as an experiment. It proved so successful that by 1896 the Royal Mint had to increase production of copper pennies threefold to meet demand.

Holmes enjoyed an easy, Bohemian existence, with his shag tobacco stuffed into the

Watson and Holmes, at home in Baker Street.

toe of a Persian slipper and his cigars stored in the coal scuttle. In a corner by the window stood a small 'acid-stained deal-topped table' littered with bottles and test tubes, where he conducted his experiments. The wooden mantelpiece was buried in a clutter of objects, including the products of his dubious habit of gathering 'all the plugs and dottles left from his smokes of the day before, carefully dried and collected on the corner'. Unanswered letters were pinioned in the centre of the mantel by a sturdy jack-knife.

Among the furnishings of 'humble lodging-house mahogany', as Watson called them, were their respective fireside chairs and a table on which Mrs Hudson placed the tray of afternoon tea. The teapot and crockery gleamed in the light of a brass, oil-filled 'student-lamp', which Holmes turned low before setting out on a case. One of the more curious items to modern eyes was the gasogene, a double sphere of glass, rather like a figure eight, and resembling a coffee percolator. Crystals in the upper globe produced gas which aerated water in the lower, like a primitive soda siphon. Victorians loved them for adding a splash of sparkling water to their whisky, but horrific cases were reported of gasogenes exploding and embedding shards of glass in the walls.

A bookcase, often a good insight into a

Holmes conducted his scientific experiments at a small 'acid-stained deal-topped table'.

Holmes, author of *Upon the Tracing of Footsteps*, examines tracings of an animal's
footmarks in *The Adventure of the Crooked Man*.

man's character, was stuffed with a wide selection, from classics to textbooks on chemistry. There was the *Life of Johnson* ('I am lost without my Boswell', Holmes joked in *A Scandal in Bohemia*); Thoreau, from which he related an anecdote when they were trout-fishing at Shoscombe; his large, well-thumbed street map of London; and almost certainly Knapp and Baldwin's four-volume, calf-bound edition of the *Newgate Calendar*, from which he acquired his knowledge of criminal cases of the century. Major Arthur Griffiths, a former H. M. Inspector of Prisons, had just published his three comprehensive volumes of *Mysteries of Police and Crime*, which would have filled in the omissions of the *Newgate Calendar*.

Among this varied collection were copies of Holmes's own published monographs, which included:

*Upon the Distinction Between the Ashes of Various Tobaccos* One hundred and forty forms of cigar, cigarette and pipe tobacco, with coloured plates illustrating the difference in ash. 'It is a point which is continu-

ally turning up in criminal trials, and which is sometimes of supreme importance as a clue', he explained to Watson. 'If you can say definitely, for example, that some murder had been done by a man who was smoking an Indian lunkah, it obviously narrows your field of search. To the trained eye there is as much difference between the black ash of a Trichinopoly and the white fluff of a bird's-eye as there is between a cabbage and a potato.'

*Upon the Tracing of Footsteps* With some remarks upon the uses of plaster of Paris as a preserver of impresses.

*Upon the Influence of a Trade Upon the Form of a Hand* With lithotypes of the hands of slaters, sailors, cork-cutters, compositors, weavers and diamond-polishers. Holmes believed the subject to be 'a matter of great practical interest to the scientific detective – especially in cases of unclaimed bodies, or in discovering the antecedents of criminals'.

*Upon the Subject of Secret Writings* 'A trifling monograph in which I analyse one hundred and sixty separate ciphers', he explained to

Watson and Inspector Martin in *The Dancing Men*.

*The Polyphonic Motets of Lassus* Printed for private circulation. According to Watson in *The Bruce-Partington Plans*, experts on these obscure medieval vocal compositions, set to words from the Scriptures, regarded Holmes's work as 'the last word upon the subject'.

*Tattoo Marks* Including a study of the pink pigment peculiar to Chinese practitioners of the art.

Holmes also contributed two short but authoritative articles to the *Anthropological Journal* on ears as a means of identification. On the shelves there was a copy of an English magazine containing a piece with the 'somewhat ambitious' heading, *The Book of Life*. Holmes tried to show in it how much could be learned by observation and systematic study of everything that came the reader's way. One of his lesser-known monographs was about the dating of documents by analysing the handwriting – a method which he claimed in *The Hound of the Baskervilles* could pinpoint the date of a manuscript to 'within a decade or so'.

In the course of the adventures he referred to other works that he planned to write on *The Chaldean Roots of the Cornish Language*, *The Use of Dogs in Detective Work*, *Malingering*, and *The Typewriter and its Relation to Crime*. When his career in private criminal investigation was over he withdrew to a south coast cottage to tend his hives, and write his *magnum opus*, *The Practical Book of Bee Culture*.

The bookcase at 221B would almost certainly have included works written by his adversaries – perhaps a copy of Prof. Moriarty's *Treatise on the Binomial Theorem*, and Col. Sebastian Moran's two books, *Heavy Game of the Western Himalayas* and the autobiographical *Three Months in the Jungle*.

There may also have been a copy of the definitive *Chinese Pottery* by Baron Gruner, the Austrian murderer in *The Illustrious Client*. Among Watson's collection was a copy of *Obscure Nervous Lesions* by Dr Percy Trevelyn, Holmes's client in *The Resident Patient*. The work, according to its author, had a certain scarcity value: 'My publishers give me a most discouraging account of its sale', he confessed to Watson. His favourite fiction is thought to have been Clark Russell's 'fine sea stories', which appeared from time to time in *Strand*.

Their Baker Street sitting-room also had a rack stacked with Holmes's pipes. He was a heavy smoker, usually found billowing out clouds of smoke when considering a problem. On a scale of difficulty the three-pipe problem required his fullest attention, which meant silence for at least fifty minutes. Holmes occasionally had a cigar or cigarette, but felt most at home with his well-worn clay, briar or long cherrywood which he used for contemplation. He would light it from a red-hot coal which he plucked from the grate with a pair of tongs. Then, for as much as a whole day, he might ramble round the room 'with his chin upon his chest and his brows knitted, charging and recharging his pipe with the strongest black tobacco . . .'

He was also immensely fond of his old, oily clay pipe. 'Having lit it', we read in *A Case of Identity*, 'he leaned back in his chair, with the thick blue cloud-wreaths spinning up from him, and a look of infinite langour in his face.'

Holmes, we must assume, possessed an iron constitution if Watson's accounts of his smoking habits are to be believed. Before breakfast – fresh rashers and eggs were a favourite – he would collect those foul dottles scraped out the night before, stuff them back into his pipe and light up, to read *The Times* agony column in his dressing-gown.

Thanks once more to unstoppable Holmesian scholarship, we know, according to the computations of John Hicks, that the detective smoked a pipe in thirty-five out of sixty stories. In only ten cases, Mr Hicks states with authority, does he smoke cigars and/or cigarettes, but not a pipe. And, for those who find such myopia irresistible, he smokes a pipe only, to the exclusion of cigars and cigarettes, in twenty-nine cases. At which rate surviving to the age of retirement was perhaps the most miraculous Holmes adventure of all.

One of the sitting-room walls had the unmistakable royal cypher V:R picked out in bullet holes. The artist was Holmes with his 'hair-trigger revolver and a box of Boxer cartridges'. On another wall hung two pictures: one newly-framed of General Gordon, beneath which Watson kept some books; the other an unframed portrait of Henry Ward Beecher, the American anti-slavery campaigner. It was on a blazing August day, as Watson sat gazing at them, that Holmes astonished him by reading his thoughts, as recorded in *The Cardboard Box*. After telling Watson exactly what he had been thinking, Holmes explained:

'... Your eyes fixed themselves upon your newly-framed picture of General Gordon, and I saw by the alteration in your face that a train of thought had started. But it did not lead very far – your eyes flashed across to the unframed portrait of Henry Ward Beecher ... Then you glanced up at the wall, and of course your meaning was obvious. You were thinking that if the portrait were framed, it would just cover that bare space and correspond with Gordon's picture over there.'

In *The Copper Beeches* Watson observes that Holmes's long cherrywood pipe 'was wont to replace his clay when he was in a disputatious, rather than a meditative mood'.

Holmes reads Watson's thoughts in *The Cardboard Box*.

'You have followed me wonderfully', Watson exclaims.

'But now your thoughts went back to Beecher, and you looked hard across as if you were studying the character of his features. Then your eyes ceased to pucker, but you continued to look across, and your face was thoughtful. You were recalling the incidents of Beecher's career. I was well aware that you could not do this without thinking of the mission which he undertook on behalf of the North at the time of the Civil War, for I remember your expressing your passionate indignation at the way in which he was received by the more turbulent of our people ... When I observed that your lips set, your eyes sparkled and your hands clenched, I was positive that you were indeed thinking of the gallantry which was shown by both sides in that desperate struggle. But then, again, your face grew sadder; you shook your head. You were dwelling upon the sadness and horror and useless waste of life ...'

'Absolutely!' Watson exclaims.

'It was all very superficial, my dear Watson, I assure you', Holmes murmurs modestly.

Holmes kept his violin case propped in the corner of the sitting-room, near to hand in case, as Watson put it, he should go 'off to violin land, where all is sweetness and delicacy'. The detective, who was a competent player, said that he preferred French and Italian music to German because they were more introspective. Music had quite an effect on Holmes, more so even than cocaine, bringing about a remarkable change in his character. In *The Red-Headed League* he persuades Watson to take an afternoon off to join him at a Sarasate concert in St James's Hall:

'... he sat in the stalls wrapped in the most perfect happiness, gently waving his long, thin fingers in time to the music, while his gently smiling face and his languid dreamy eyes were as unlike Holmes the sleuth hound, Holmes the relentless ... as it was possible to conceive.'

His own instrument was a Stradivarius,

worth at least 500 guineas, and bought from a Tottenham Court Road pawnshop for 55 shillings. Lubricated with a little wine, he could tell 'anecdote after anecdote' about his idol, Paganini, who also played one. Holmes composed his own music, often playing in a curious style with the fiddle across his knee, while he mulled over a particular problem.

Their sitting-room was a consulting-room, a place for relaxation with bundles of manuscripts and scattered newspapers (Holmes took *The Times*, and went out for the *Daily Telegraph* if he wanted to look up something) – and also a room full of memories. Souvenirs from great cases could be found here and there. There was probably the wax bust of himself, with the bullet hole through the forehead, fashioned to trap Col. Sebastian Moran. The photograph of Irene Adler, the first and last woman to get the better of him. And, still in active service, the long, thin walking-cane he had used to attack the swamp adder in *The Speckled Band*. Watson, a well-travelled ex-military man (5th Northumberland Fusiliers, then attached to the Berkshires) might have picked up one or two mementoes of the Second Afghan War before he was invalided out with a bullet in the shoulder.

## S. Holmes, Consulting Detective – Discretion Guaranteed

HOLMES RECEIVED HIS clients in the sitting-room while Watson occasionally discreetly withdrew to his bedroom to ensure their privacy. It is not clear what they made of the great man, or indeed what they had been led to expect. Like any professional Holmes was not allowed to advertise his services. He attracted cases by recommendation, while his reputation was, of course, spread by Watson's published stories.

His roots in the squirearchy meant, to some extent, he was a gentleman of means, but he obviously had to earn a living. Holmes the self-employed businessman veered from the ruthless to the erratic, charging high fees to one client while refusing anything from another. Those who tramped wearily up the stairs to the sitting-room of 221B came from all levels of society, but Holmes – who displayed the qualities of Victorian liberalism – was unimpressed by rank or status. Indeed, he 'loathed every form of Society with his whole Bohemian

Music had a remarkable effect on Holmes.

soul,' Watson tells us in *A Scandal in Bohemia*. It was one of his great redeeming features; an unexpectedly human quality beneath the calculating machine.

Holmes was an extremely complex and contradictory character, a tribute to Conan Doyle's skill at compressing both the scope and detail of a novel into short story form.

Professionally he had an easy courtesy which made even the most fraught client relax and talk in the homely disorder of his consulting-room. For a man who had poured so much into training and acquiring specialized knowledge, his career appeared to completely lack direction – a fact perhaps not unconnected with his fatalistic view of life. Watson could not help observing the absence of an overall scheme – his friend was happy to be successful with each case rather than expand his practice. Holmes, he tells us, could be found 'alternating from week to week between cocaine and ambition, the drowsiness of the drug and the fierce energy of his own keen nature'. Had he been taken in hand by an ambitious woman, who knows what different picture might have emerged – Holmes International plc? Perhaps we should be thankful for his bachelor Bohemianism.

He was, however, not as carefree about fees as his devil-may-care nature suggests. ('My professional charges are on a fixed scale – I do not vary them, save when I remit them altogether.') Holmes wasted no time getting down to business with the King of Bohemia, for instance:

'Then as to money?'

'You have carte blanche.'

'Absolutely?' he insists, to make his position doubly sure.

'And for present expenses?'

At this point the King takes a heavy

Holmes calms down a distraught client in *The Beryl Coronet*.

Holmes kept records of every case he had worked on in a large tin chest.

chamois leather bag and counts out £300 in gold and £700 in notes. Holmes took the payment and 'scribbled a receipt'.

The King gave him a bonus of a 'snuff box of old gold with a great amethyst in the centre of the lid'. Holmes also wore a valuable ring which sparkled on his finger. When Watson tackled him about it, he shrugged off the inquiries: 'It was from the reigning family of Holland, though the matter in which I served them was of such delicacy that I cannot confide.' Queen Victoria, we are told, presented him with an emerald tie pin at Windsor in recognition of services rendered.

Holmes was extremely shrewd when it came to settling fees for his work. After recovering the precious stones in *The Beryl Coronet*, for instance, he secures his payment before he hands over the gems. He first ensures that he receives the money he had to pay out to get them back, then adds his fee on top:

'Three thousand will cover the matter. And there is a little reward, I fancy. Have you your chequebook? Here is a pen. Better make it out for four thousand pounds.'

We can safely assume that he lost no time putting it into his bank account. In the closing paragraph of *His Last Bow* he jumps into the car and orders: 'Start her up, Watson, for it's time that we were on our way. I have a cheque for five hundred pounds which should be cashed early, for the drawer is quite capable of stopping it, if he can.'

His earnings were considerable, enabling him to travel everywhere first class and support an expensive cocaine habit. Yet he preferred to share lodgings for the companionship and simple lifestyle. Money to Holmes was no more than a means of supporting himself; his real riches came from the higher things it could not buy.

The haphazard daily life of 221B was a sharp contrast to Holmes's precise and systematic investigating techniques. He equipped himself for every eventuality with a variety of eccentric tools – from his low-powered microscope to the dark lantern he used in *The Red-Headed League*, which could vary its output of light. At the heart of the paraphernalia was a filing system, intricately cross-indexed, to provide instant access to information.

'For many years he had adopted a system of docketing all paragraphs concerning men and things, so that it was difficult to name a subject or a person on which he could not at once furnish information', Watson tells us.

Conan Doyle possibly obtained the idea from Newnes's comprehensive press-cuttings library at Southampton Street. *Tit-Bits*, for many years, was written entirely from press cuttings, either collected by staff or sent in by readers, and provided a formidable wealth of knowledge. Information became an obsession with the Victorian reading public, and private cuttings libraries were started by individuals as a hobby.

It is interesting, incidentally, that William Baring-Gould, author of *The Annotated Sherlock Holmes*, notes that many cataloguing experts have sniggered at Holmes's filing methods. In *The Sussex Vampire*, for example, he takes down his great index book and runs his finger down the letter 'V', reading out subjects which catch his eye:

Voyage of the *Gloria Scott*
Victor Lynch, the forger
Venomous lizard, or gila
Vittoria, the circus belle
Venderbilt and the Yeggman
Vipers
Vigor, the Hammersmith wonder
Vampirism in Hungary

He indexed topics as he remembered them, not in strict and tedious alphabetical order. And, despite the experts' cynicism there was nothing unusual in the method.

Many of Holmes's cuttings were pasted in his Commonplace Book ('I read nothing except the criminal news and the agony column', he once said, though this was not quite true). In a private diary he kept a record of case histories. The filing method was so complex that it needed frequent attention, a task he tended to put off until the fancy took him. In *The Five Orange Pips* he 'sat moodily at one side of the fireplace cross-indexing his records of crime'.

At the scene of a crime he took in the stage and the leading characters at a glance, rarely telling Watson what was going through his mind. If something required closer examination he would take out the magnifying glass which generations of illustrators and cartoonists associated with him. In *A Study in Scarlet* we find Holmes brandishing his lens in full eccentric cry:

'He whipped a tape measure and a large round magnifying glass from his pocket. With these two implements he trotted noiselessly about the room, sometimes stopping, occasionally kneeling, and once lying flat upon his face. So engrossed was he with this occupation that he appeared to have forgotten our presence, for he chattered away to himself under his breath the whole time, keeping up a running fire of exclamations, groans, whistles and little cries . . .'

Whether this extravagant performance was to impress Inspectors Gregson and Lestrade of Scotland Yard is unclear. But they 'watched the manoeuvres of their amateur

Inspector Lestrade of Scotland Yard, a 'lean, ferret-like man, furtive and sly-looking',
uncovers a vital piece of information in *A Study in Scarlet*.

companion with considerable curiosity and contempt'.

Holmes had a long-running love-hate relationship with the Yard's detectives. He had as little regard for their methods as they had for his, and particularly disliked the way in which they took the glory for his inspired groundwork. In this same incident, when they ask his opinion, he replies with heavy sarcasm: 'It would rob you of the credit of the case if I was to presume to help you. You are doing so well now that it would be a pity for anyone to interfere.'

We can infer from this, and similar tart replies, that Holmes had more than a touch of the *prima donna* concerning his work. He did not suffer fools gladly, and he treated anyone of lesser intelligence rather brusquely. The police, portrayed by Conan Doyle as plodding and a trifle pompous, fall squarely into this category. Mr Jones of Scotland Yard sums up the official view of Holmes when he patronizingly says in *The Red-Headed League*; 'He has his own methods which are, if he won't mind my saying so, just a little too theoretical and fantastic, but he has the makings of a detective in him.'

Inspector Lestrade, 'the pick of a bad lot', is less restrained. 'I've wasted time enough', he remonstrates, rising to his feet, in *The Noble Bachelor*. 'I believe in hard work, and not in sitting by the fire spinning fine theories. Good day, Mr Holmes and we shall see who gets to the bottom of the matter first.' As he leaves he shoots a pitying glance at Holmes. Then, turning to Watson, taps his forehead with his finger and shakes his head solemnly.

Despite the friction, Holmes was on better terms with Lestrade than any of the other Yard officers. There was a hint of friendliness in their banter but, though their working relationship became quite close, the pair could never reconcile themselves to

each other's methods. 'That imbecile Lestrade!' Holmes calls him in *The Boscombe Valley Mystery*.

Watson was not entirely taken with him either. 'A lean, ferret-like man, furtive and sly-looking was waiting for us upon the platform ... I had no difficulty in recognising Lestrade of Scotland Yard.' There was a keen, often caustic competitiveness between Holmes and his opposite numbers, and their exchanges were on many occasions loaded with mutual contempt. 'Theories are all very well', Lestrade says, 'but *we* have to deal with a hard-headed British jury.' For Holmes, who thrived on recognition (he was 'as sensitive to flattery on the score of his art as any girl would be of her beauty'), denegration of his methods was not only an insult, but the mark of a buffoon. His responses varied from seething anger to self-deprecating good humour, depending how the mood took him. When the police refused to take his client's problem seriously in *The Five Orange Pips*, Holmes shook his clenched hands in the air with rage. 'Incredible imbecility!' he shouted.

Lestrade grew to respect the consulting detective's success rate, and, of course, the honours it brought him for appearing to have solved the crime. By the time they collaborated on *The Hound of the Baskervilles*, Watson noted a change; 'I saw at once from the reverential way in which Lestrade gazed at my companion that he had learned a good deal since the days when they had first worked together.' Indeed, Lestrade woud even call on Holmes when a case was difficult, flop in the chair at 221B and confess; 'I can neither make head nor tail of this business'.

Patronizing as the Yard were, it was easy to see why they lost their patience with Holmes. Here was a well-paid private detective, picking only cases which interested him, tramping over clues and interfering with evidence, while they tried to carry out their duty. It was not so much Holmes's methods – they were seen as merely whimsical – but his secretiveness, which annoyed them. In addition, he had an irritating habit of pointing out clues without explaining how they were linked to the crime – often, it seemed, for his own amusement.

also from his professional caution, which urged him never to take any chances. The result, however, was very trying for those who were acting as his agents and assistants.'

Holmes's attitude to justice and the law did little to cement his relationship with the Force. He was not above turning a blind eye to letting an offender escape if, in his view, justice had been done. He was also

Officers at the Yard disapproved of Holmes's unorthodox methods, despite his high success rate.

Lestrade summed up their feelings in *The Norwood Builder:* 'I don't know whether you are playing a game with us, Mr Sherlock Holmes. If you know anything, you can surely say it without all this tomfoolery.'

Watson also felt a victim of his stubborn insularity: 'One of Sherlock Holmes's defects – if indeed one may call it a defect,' he tells us in *The Hound of the Baskervilles,* 'was that he was exceedingly loth to communicate his full plans to any other person until the instant of their fulfilment. Partly it came no doubt from his own masterful nature which loved to dominate and surprise those who were around him. Partly

not averse to breaking the law himself in the course of his inquiries – cutting corners which the police could not. The reward lay in bringing cases to a swift and satisfactory conclusion; the penalty, in watching lumbering gentlemen of the Yard get the kudos. The fact that the Press were influenced by official statements must have made Holmes feel grateful for Watson's published accounts of his adventures.

The *Echo,* reporting the events of *A Study in Scarlet,* concluded: 'It is an open secret that the credit of this smart capture belongs entirely to the well-known Scotland Yard officers, Messrs Lestrade and Gregson. The

Lestrade and Holmes try to restrain their prisoner in *A Study in Scarlet*.

man was apprehended, it appears, in the rooms of a certain Mr Sherlock Holmes, who has himself, as an amateur, shown some talent in the detective line, and who, with such instructors, may hope in time to attain to some degree of their skill . . .'

Holmes took it phlegmatically. He believed that he was not conceited about success. 'If I claim full justice for my art', he explained in *The Copper Beeches*, 'it is because it is an impersonal thing – a thing beyond itself. Crime is common. Logic is rare.'

## The Noble Bachelor

WHEN HOLMES IS FIRST introduced to his new flatmate at the beginning of *A Study in Scarlet*, he good-humouredly warns Watson that he smokes shag tobacco and dabbles with chemicals. 'Let me see – what are my other short-comings? I get in the dumps at times, and don't open my mouth for days on end. You must not think I am sulky when I do that. Just let me alone, and I'll soon be right . . .'

The doctor discovered that there were other shortcomings, but the odd couple became firm friends. Holmes, despite his rather frigid idiosyncracies, grew very fond of 'good old Watson'. He may not have possessed the detective's incisive mind, but he was loyal and reliable, a good man to have in a tight corner. When Watson arrived by train in *The Boscombe Valley Mystery*, Holmes, pacing the platorm was relieved to see him: 'It is really very good of you to come, Watson. It makes a considerable difference to me, having someone with me on whom I can thoroughly rely.'

So much so that, beneath his cool exterior, Holmes valued Watson's companionship more than he cared to admit. Peeling away the veneers of professional formality,

secrecy and sarcasm, through which he distanced himself, we find a man of very human emotions. Conan Doyle buried them deep, but they are there, nonetheless. Holmes the self-sufficient adventurer would have found life very empty without his pedestrian friend. It was only when there was a real risk of losing him that his true feelings surfaced. Watson took a revolver bullet in the thigh in *The Three Garridebs*. Holmes instantly dealt with the attacker, 'then my friends arms were round me and he was leading me to a chair'.

' "You're not hurt, Watson? For God's sake say that you are not hurt!"

'It was worth a wound – it was worth many wounds – to know the depth of loyalty and love which lay behind that cold mask. The clear, hard eyes were dimmed for a moment, and the firm lips were shaking. For the one and only time I caught a glimpse of a great heart as well as of a great brain . . . His face set like flint as he glared at our prisoner who was sitting up with a dazed face.

"By the Lord, it is as well for you. If you had killed Watson, you would not have got out of this room alive." '

It is, of course, the stuff of heroes – firm of jaw and true of heart. At least it would appear so. But Holmes under his normal composure left the good doctor in little doubt of his function in their relationship. In *The Creeping Man* Watson gives a rare account of how, beneath the simple, bluff exterior, he had Holmes quite firmly in perspective.

'He was a man of habits', he tells us, 'narrow and conceited habits, and I had become one of them. As an institution I was like the violin, the shag tobacco, the old black pipe, the index books, and others perhaps less excusable. When it was a case of active work and a comrade was needed

'Good old Watson' comes to Holmes's rescue in *The Reigate Squire*.

upon whose nerve he could place some reliance, my role was obvious. But apart from this I had uses. I was a whetstone for his mind. I stimulated him. He liked to think aloud in my presence. His remarks could hardly be said to be made to me – many of them would have been as appropriately addressed to his bedstead – but none the less, having formed the habit, it had become in some way helpful that I should register and interject. If I irritated him by a certain methodical slowness in my mentality, that irritation served only to make his own flame-like intuitions and impressions flash up the more vividly and swiftly. Such was my humble role in our alliance.'

Poor old Watson; but there were compensations. The action, danger and constant sense of living close to the madness made life at 221B appealing to an ex-military man obliged to seek his livelihood as a humdrum GP. When the time came Watson found no difficulty in departing for the fresh pastures of domesticity and marriage, but Holmes had no such comforts to console his restless spirit. He withdrew into his hard shell and devoted himself to the Method which held him more firmly than any religion.

The actor William Gillette in the role of Sherlock Holmes as drawn by the cartoonist Spy in
*Vanity Fair* (1907).

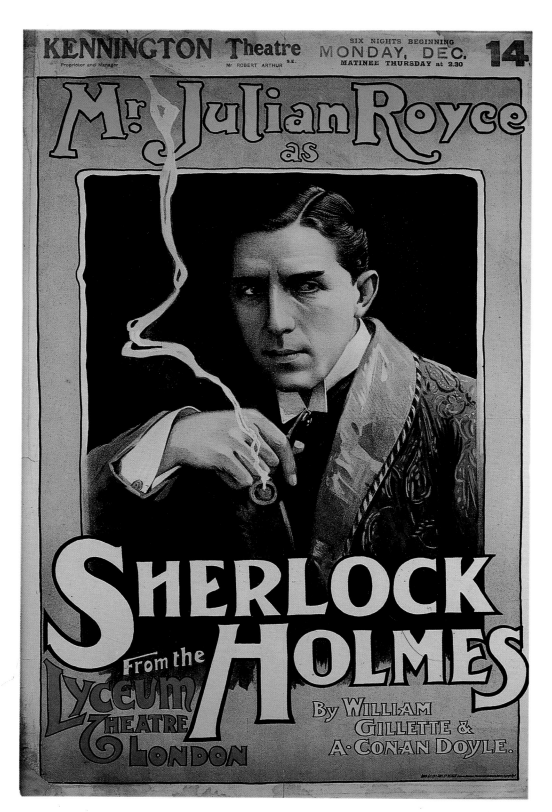

A tour poster of William Gillette's play *Sherlock Holmes,* based on the Holmes stories of Conan Doyle, with Julian Royce in the lead role.

Their friendship was founded on the attraction of opposites. Watson, on the whole, was made of more durable stuff. His resilience stemmed from a natural inclination to give and take. Holmes found reciprocation uncomfortable, even in the smallest things. 'It was one of the peculiarities of his proud, self-contained nature that, though he docketed any fresh information very quickly and accurately in his brain, he seldom made any acknowledgement to the giver.' Against the wise understanding of Watson, it indicated a weaker character.

Holmes ultimately suffered for his exclusive devotion to his art. Watson, who had the stamina of a bull terrier, frequently referred to Holmes's iron constitution, but there were times when the detective cracked under the strain of his lop-sided lifestyle. By April 1887 he was bedridden with nervous exhaustion in a French hotel. He had worked on a case for two months, often for up to fifteen hours a day, which had resulted in his reputation spreading throughout Europe, and left the Baker Street door mat 'ankle deep with congratulatory telegrams'. The great man himself, meanwhile, was recovering from a breakdown and severe depression.

Physically he was immensely strong – capable of bending a steel poker with his bare hands – and extremely fit, despite his heavy smoking habits. He was an expert fencer, an enthusiastic amateur boxer who could handle himself well, and a formidable opponent with a singlestick – a heavy cane used in sabre practice, but more frequently for street fighting. Only his eyesight appears to have been slightly impaired, judging by the number of occasions he hands a paper to Watson and asks: 'Would you read it to me aloud.'

Holmes's robust constitution is something of a mystery, for he had little regard for diet – especially when working – and often looked haggard and drawn. In *The Five Orange Pips* he returned home 'looking pale and worn. He walked up to the sideboard and, tearing a piece from the loaf, he devoured it voraciously, washing it down with a long draught of water.'

'You are hungry?' Watson asks rather unnecessarily.

'Starving. It had escaped my memory. I have had nothing since breakfast.'

Disregard for his health, and the tight rein he kept on his emotions, left him with a range of nervous mannerisms – the habit of rubbing his fingers together, throwing himself into chairs, and pacing restlessly up and

Holmes, deep in thought.

Holmes and Moriarty: the thin line between good and evil.

down the sitting-room. We have no description of the carpet, but it was presumably quite threadbare in patches. When he was excited he tended to wriggle in his chair, like a schoolboy; when thoughtful he would draw his boney knees in a foetal position up to his hawk-like nose and close his eyes. He had a high-pitched voice, we learn in *The Stockbroker's Clerk*, and a tooth missing from a fight in *The Empty House*. At least one Holmesian expert adds to this a rather disturbing yellow smile from all that shag tobacco, which must have stained his teeth. But with Holmes's meticulous personal habits this was perhaps carrying realism too far.

'Sherlock Holmes was a man who seldom took exercise for exercise's sake,' Watson tells us in *The Silver Blaze*. 'Few men were capable of greater muscle effort ... but he looked upon aimless bodily exertion as a waste of energy ... That he should have kept himself in training under such circumstances is remarkable.'

One saving grace was his humour, mischievous and a little forced at times, but giving nevertheless some spark of spontaneity to the impression of a walking calculator. Watson found his ideas of humour 'strange and occasionally offensive'. In *The Mazarin Stone* they were even considered 'somewhat perverse'. All were based, however, on an engaging philosophy that 'life is full of whimsical happenings'. And in the strange world of Sherlock Holmes it is a sentiment few would disagree with.

The Master, as Holmesians reverentially refer to the great detective, was the great Victorian hero – fearless, brilliant, ready to grasp life firmly by the lapels and, of course, British into the bargain. Not the blind patriot, but a reasoning man with a rounded view of the world. A man with a sense of common justice in a society besieged by lawlessness. A champion who turned every suburban reader's sense of indignation into action; who boldly went forth to show the well-intentioned but painfully slow police how it should be done.

On the surface Sherlock Holmes reads like Superman. But Conan Doyle, a master of his craft, sketched deep perspectives of arrogance and uncertainty which made him a flawed, but enduring, hero. There are those who strive to make him something different; those who play the game of pretending that Watson, not Doyle, wrote the stories. But Holmes is lovable because he *is* such a gawky, brilliant eccentric acting like a *Boy's Own* hero. In his more erratic moments he strayed dangerously down the path of Prof. Moriarty – an inspired mind blinded by its own brilliance.

Holmes himself admitted that the line between the crook and the detective was a thin one: 'It is fortunate for this community that I am not a criminal ...' Only his immense capacity for reasoning – and the stabilizing influence of Watson – prevented him from becoming the real Napoleon of Crime.

## Good Old Watson

WATSON'S GENIAL, down-to-earth personality loomed large in Holmes's life, obligingly adopting roles suited to his oscillating moods. Watson was alternately the slow-witted fool, loyal partner, personal physician and father confessor. To whom else could Holmes admit, when the pressure was on: 'It's all going wrong, Watson – all as wrong as it can go ...'

Watson was an uncomplicated companion with simple needs. He had a capacity, too, to organize his life in a way that eluded the late-rising, untidy detective. For much of their time together he ran a busy practice and, after a hard day at surgery, cheerfully coped with his unpredictable friend. Calls on his services were heavy in *A Case of Identity*: 'A professional case of great gravity was engaging my own attention at the time, and the whole of the next day I was busy at the bedside of the sufferer. It was not until six o'clock that I found myself free ...'

He was fortunate to marry a woman of equal understanding. In *The Boscombe Valley Mystery*, for instance, he discusses his long list of patients with her, but she encourages him to assist Holmes. It was such evenness and stability that Holmes came to depend on. Watson became an indispensable companion and, when danger threatened, Holmes would sometimes dissuade him from tagging along, for his own safety.

It is a measure of Watson's character that he built a thriving practice while trying to support his friend. He had purchased it from Farquhar, an elderly Paddington doctor suffering from St Vitus's Dance. Because of his infirmity patients had fallen from 1,200 a year to 300, but Watson saw it as a worthy challenge to which to devote his energies.

He remarried when his first wife died and remained a devoted, uncomplaining husband. His war wound gave him gyp in damp weather, but he rarely burdened others with his troubles. In *The Noble Bachelor* he recalls: 'I had remained indoors all day, for the weather had taken a sudden turn to rain, with high autumnal winds, and the Jezail bullet which I had brought back in one of my limbs as a relic of my Afghan campaign, throbbed with a dull persistency . . .'

Watson had a way with the ladies, and Holmes often called on his charm to smooth awkward situations – 'the fair sex is your department' he told him. This has inflamed the imagination of Holmesian scholars to a fever of tabloid newspaper proportions. Why, they ask, was he transferred from his own army brigade to the Berkshires during military service? 'There remains only one possible explanation', said the late Dr Ernest Bloomfield Zeisler. 'Watson had contracted venereal disease, either syphilis or gonorrhea, both of which were always common in and about military establishments in those days.' Watson may once have remarked that he possessed 'an experience of women which extends over many nations and three separate continents', but

we must allow him the privilege of wishful thinking. The stigma of sexually transmitted disease is undeserved for a disabled ex-officer of the 5th Northumberland who served Queen and country.

When Watson enters the first Holmes story, *A Study in Scarlet*, it is, curiously, in similar circumstances to those Doyle experienced on leaving the insufferable Budds. 'Worn with pain and weak from the prolonged hardships' of his war service, he moved into a private hotel in the Strand, 'leading a comfortless meaningless existence and spending such money as I had, considerably more freely than I ought'. It was at this point that he ran into Stamford, an ex-student, at the Criterion Bar – the meeting which led to his introduction to Holmes. Both were drawn by the need for companionship as much as cheap accommodation. 'By Jove!' Watson exclaims on hearing that Holmes needs a flatmate. '. . . I am the very man for him. I should prefer having a partner to being alone.'

Watson was an uncomplicated companion with simple needs.

His spending money more freely than he ought has often raised the question of Watson's gambling. The first hint that he might be a gaming man came later in *A Study in Scarlet*. He read a magazine article – little knowing that Holmes had written it – claiming that the author could identify a man's trade by looking at him. 'I would lay a thousand to one against him', Watson splutters. An innocent enough expression in itself, but by the time they are investigating the case of *The Dancing Men*, Watson's cheque-book is safely locked in Holmes's desk drawer, with the arrangement that he has to ask for the key to use it. As time goes by we find him ruefully telling Holmes, in *Shoscombe Old Place*, that 'about half my wound pension' was spent on the Turf.

For a man who held few people in any high regard – if we discount Queen Victoria and Paganini – Holmes had great admiration for Watson. 'I never get your limits', he once told hin. 'There are unexplored possibilities about you.'

The good doctor, in turn, treated his friend with the utmost respect of someone who could see both strengths and weaknesses. The detective, he swore, was 'the best and wisest man whom I have ever known'. Yet, when Watson married, there was a sense of disappointment in Holmes. His old prejudices intruded and they began to spend less time together. 'He still came to me from time to time when he desired a companion for his investigations,' Watson recalled, 'but these occasions grew more and more seldom, until I find that in the year 1890 there were only three cases of which I retain any record.

It had been a trying association, even for such an agreeable fellow as Watson. Holmes's offhandedness would have tested the greatest patience. But even when he came out with remarks such as: 'I wish you simply to report facts in the fullest possible manner to me, and you can leave me to do the reasoning', the doctor never bridled. They were passing irritations which a man of character would ignore.

Their eventual parting was Holmes's loss. In *The Hound of the Baskervilles* he pushed back his chair, lit a cigarette, and paid Watson a rare and glowing tribute; '. . . you are a conductor of light. Some people, without possessing genius, have a remarkable power of stimulating it. I confess, my dear fellow, that I am very much in your debt.'

Few readers who enjoy the adventures could fail to add Holmes's famous remark: 'Good old Watson! You are the one fixed point in a changing age.'

# The Mysterious Mycroft Holmes

MYCROFT, HOLMES'S OLDER brother, drifts mysteriously through the stories like river fog rolling through Limehouse. He was a curious, slightly sinister figure betraying only a little of the immense power he wielded in the corridors of Whitehall. On the surface he led a very mundane life, leaving his Pall Mall rooms only to go to work or cross the road to the Diogenes Club, which he had a hand in founding. It catered for 'the most unsociable, unclubbable' men in London, and one of its rules was that no member should take the slightest notice of another. Talking was not permitted, except in the Strangers Room, where visitors could be received.

It was here that Watson first met Mycroft – 'A much larger and stouter man than Sherlock. His body was absolutely corpulent, but his face, though massive, had preserved something of the sharpness of expression which was so remarkable in that

Mycroft Holmes pays a visit to 221B Baker Street in *The Greek Interpreter*.

of his brother. His eyes, which were of a peculiarly light, watery grey, seemed to always retain that far away, introspective look which I had only observed in Sherlock's when he was exerting his full powers.'

Mycroft was the archetypal Whitehall mandarin; a man whose life was spent keeping secrets. Knowing that his discretion was guaranteed, Holmes asked his brother, rather than Watson, to keep 221B in order, and send him money, when he went to ground after the Reichenbach Falls incident. When Holmes was back in residence, Mycroft rarely visited Baker Street. Because of the mystery surrounding the detective's travels, and the fact that he assumed the identity of a Norwegian named Sigerson, it has been supposed that he was perhaps working for the Foreign Office

abroad, and reporting back to Mycroft.

It was Mycroft, too, who held the only clue to Holmes's early life, a subject which he did not discuss, even with Watson.

Only once did Holmes lift the veil on his brother's true activities. Far from merely auditing books in Whitehall departments – an image he preferred to encourage – he actively controlled government policy. In *The Bruce-Partington Plans* Holmes explains:

'The conclusions of every department are passed to him, and he is the central exhange, the clearing house, which makes out the balance. All other men are specialists, but his specialism is omniscience. We will suppose that a Minister needs information as to a point which involves the Navy, India, Canada and the bi-metallic question; he could get his separate advices from various departments upon each, but only Mycroft can focus them all, and say off-hand how each factor would affect the other. They began by using him as a short-cut, a convenience; now he has made himself an essential. In that great brain of his everything is pigeon-holed, and can be handed out in an instant. Again and again his word has decided the national policy. He lives in it. He thinks of nothing else, save when, as an intellectual exercise, he unbends if I call upon him and ask him to advise me on one of my little problems.'

Today, Mycroft would have been superceded by an IBM computer; in Victorian times he was an indispensable genius, demonstrating a family trait of reasoning and deduction. When Sherlock and Mycroft are seen together it seems, too, that other characteristics run in the Holmes's family blood – preoccupation with work, obsessive secrecy and an aversion to female company. They bred strange folk on those remote, mist-shrouded Yorkshire moors.

# PART III
# Sherlock Holmes
# and the
# Victorian Underworld

The Strand by gaslight.

# Crime, Detection and London Street Life

SLIPPING BETWEEN THE moonlight and shadows, a tall figure pauses at the door of the great house and stoops over the lock. A tiny circle of light from the bull's eye of his lantern gleams briefly on a bunch of skeleton keys. An instant later he is inside. A glimpse of the rising tide of Victorian crime? Burglary amounted to almost 75 per cent of offences. But there is an equal chance that it was not a cracksman, as Victorians called them, but the world's first consulting detective at work.

Holmes had no qualms about breaking and entering, and possessed a set of burglar's tools which would have been the envy of the 'darker recesses of the underworld'. He had many narrow escapes in the course of his highly irregular investigations; in *The Illustrious Client* he was threatened with prosecution for burglary, but the outcome of the case saved him appearing in the dock. Holmes went well equipped on his moonlight expeditions with his instruments, shining and well-maintained, in a neat leather case.

'This is a first-class, up-to-date burgling kit, with nickel-plated jemmy, diamond-tipped glass cutter, adaptable keys, and every modern improvement which the march of civilisation demands', he told Watson proudly in *Charles Augustus Milverton*. 'Here, too, is my dark lantern. Everything is in order. Have you a pair of silent shoes?'

'I have rubber-soled tennis shoes', Watson replies.

'Excellent. And a mask?'

'I can make a couple out of black silk ...'

Holmes's kit was compact and lightweight – perhaps not as extensive as the tools carried by Victorian professional burglars – but more than adequate for the task.

In *The Illustrious Client* he spoke fondly of 'my old friend Charlie Peace', whom he describes as a violin virtuoso. It was partly a tongue-in-cheek remark; Peace, the most notorious burglar of the era, was a keen musician, but as a youngster had appeared on a London music hall bill as The Modern Paganini, playing a single-string violin in the style of G. H. Chirgwin, The White-Eyed Kaffir. Peace's tools, now in Scotland Yard's Black Museum, were precision instruments.

'His jemmy, a little beauty, is a neat bar of polished steel', one privileged Home Office visitor noted. 'He used a small vice for turning from the far side any key which had been imprudently left in the door; also a gouge, or rather a large gimlet, and a small "bit" not three inches long, with three sharp steel teeth good enough to penetrate any woodwork, and workable with the palm of the hand. Peace's folding ladder is a triumph of simplicity. When closed it looks like a bundle of sticks in short lengths, but it can be expanded like a lazy tongs upwards to a height of twelve feet; the top carries a hook to catch on to a window ledge or any projection.'

Other 'portico thieves', whose method was to climb in through upper windows, usually carried long rope-ladders with flat wooden rungs which could be rolled and carried in an overcoat pocket. Holmes

Charles Peace, a notorious Victorian burglar.

appeared to have no special way of carrying his tools – he warned Watson not to drop them in *The Bruce-Partington Plans* – but there were waistcoats, specially tailored for the purpose, run up in East End sewing-rooms. They contained rows of patch pockets, in various shapes and sizes, into which crowbars, drills, saws, hammers, mallets, skeleton keys and clasp-knives could be slotted.

These were the basic tools of the trade catalogued by Mr Chesterton, governor of Coldbath Fields prison in the middle of the nineteenth century, and used by 'the best burglars of the day'. Some were special adaptations of handyman's tools. Crowbars, for instance, had one end sharpened like a chisel for forcing windows and trunks. Iron chests – popular for storing cash and documents – were forced by holding a strip of thick leather across the line where the lid

met the chest, and driving the crowbar into it. The soft, and noiseless, wedge lifted the lid enough for the crowbar to be inserted to force it open.

Drills were used to bore holes in door panels close to the beading. A sharp knife could then be run from hole to hole until the panel fell out. If a lock proved too stubborn or sophisticated, a hole was drilled above it and the cracksman used his keyhole saw to remove the mechanism completely. Skeleton keys, or picklocks as they were called, were used on desk drawers, cupboards and safes. An essential part of the kit was a small bottle of prussic acid or nux vomica ('ox-vomit' in underworld slang) to silence guard dogs swiftly.

The famous dark lantern, which Holmes used while lying in wait for the gang breaking through the cellar in *The Red-Headed League*, was indispensable. Towards the

Peace, like many burglars of the time, carried a gun and was prepared to use it if necessary. However, in spite of serious injuries, the courageous constable managed to bring Peace to justice.

1890s they were small and easily concealed, with a bull's eye lens which could throw a pencil-thin beam of light onto a lock, or be closed with a simple movement of the thumb. One dark lantern left at the scene of a burglary just before the turn of the century was found to be home-made from a tin match-box, with a carrying handle to protect the owner's hand from the heat of the candle.

Many of these rasping saws and clanging hammers could, of course, only be used if the house was empty. Some burglars, including Charles Peace, carried a revolver in case they were disturbed. All carried a short, heavy club, or 'life-preserver'.

Holmes believed that Peace possessed the complex mind of all great criminals. The accuracy of this remark is uncertain, but Peace was certainly a very determined and dangerous individual. His long career ended only by chance in 1878 when he was disturbed by a patrolling constable late one November night as he broke into a house in St John's Park, Blackheath. Without hesitation Peace drew his revolver and fired five shots at the officer, seriously wounding him. The constable, a man of tremendous courage, tackled Peace, who was quite small, and brought him down. As they grappled on the ground the burglar tried to finish him off with a sheath knife. The constable, incredibly, managed to arrest him and take him into custody.

In the light of the police station Peace was mistaken for a foreigner. He had dark skin and claimed to be American. Officers studying the prisoner closely discovered that he had stained his face with walnut juice, to be less detectable in the dark. It took two week's intensive inquiries to find that the man they had caught was called Johnson and came from a well-to-do part of Peckham. Peace had covered his tracks well – a search of the house revealed that Johnson was, in fact, someone called Ward, and Ward in turn was Peace – wanted all over Britain for a murder in Sheffield a year earlier.

The house was opulently furnished with valuable stolen goods – there was a 60 guinea walnut suite in the drawing-room,

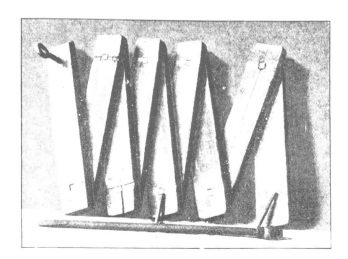

Peace's folding ladder.

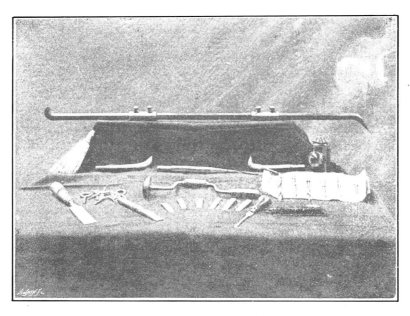

A first-class burgling kit.

gilded mirrors, a priceless Turkish carpet and, as Holmes suggested, evidence of Peace's love of music. Around the room officers found an expensive bijou piano, an inlaid Spanish guitar stolen from a titled lady, and a magnificent collection of Cremona violins which he had selectively plundered from great houses.

Holmes 'prattled away about Cremona fiddles' in *A Study in Scarlet*, which was written seven years after Peace hanged for the Sheffield murder. It was perhaps no accident that the detective mentions his 'old friend Charlie Peace'. The burglar's arrest was sensational news and Doyle must have been familiar with all the background stories which began appearing about the master criminal's methods. There are, incidentally, some interesting similarities between Holmes's break-in techniques and those of Peace. The cracksman was unusual among Victorian burglars in that he always insisted on working alone, a method

preferred by Holmes himself, save for the occasions when Watson nervously acted as look-out. Possibly the most intriguing style they shared was the use of disguise. It was rare among common criminals, and found only among a handful with a certain flair for the profession.

Peace had bases around the country – from Hull he raided wealthy homes in the East Riding; from Nottingham he broke into the silk warehouses of the East Midlands. In London he owned houses including property in Lambeth, Greenwich and Peckham, overflowing with stolen goods and housing costumes for the various identities he assumed in each. In Greenwich, for instance, he was an upper-class gentleman of private means; in Peckham a venerated old churchwarden; elsewhere a disabled man with a hook instead of a left hand.

In *The Adventure of Black Peter*, Watson tells us: 'Holmes was working somewhere under one of the numerous disguises and names with which he concealed his own formidable identity. He had at least five small refuges in different parts of London in which he was able to change his personality.'

He popped up throughout the stories dressed variously as a sailor, an Italian *A Scandal in Bohemia*, and an 'elderly deformed man' clutching a copy of *The Origin of Tree Worship* in *The Empty House*. 'It was not merely that Holmes changed his costume', Watson tells us. 'His expresison, his manner, his very soul seemed to vary with every fresh part that he assumed. The stage lost a fine actor, even as science lost an

Holmes disguised as a drunken groom.

priest, Mr Escott the plumber, an American spy of Irish extraction called Altamont, and a drunken groom. In the East End he was familiar as Captain Basil, and at least two of his disguises bore passing resemblance to those of Charles Peace: the 'aimiable and simple-minded' non-conformist preacher in acute reasoner, when he became a specialist in crime.'

Peace and Holmes also shared, coincidentally, a frank outspokenness and wry sense of humour. Peace told his jailers: 'When I was Mr Johnson of Peckham, I went into the chemist's shop one morning smoking an excellent cigar.

'The chemist observed: "That is a very good tobacco, Mr Johnson. Where do you get your cigars?"

'"Steal them," I replied, perfectly frankly and truthfully. It was the absolute fact. I had stolen those cigars. But my friend the chemist thought it an excellent joke. He roared with laughter and, of course, did not believe me in the least.

'"I wish you'd steal me a few of the same kind," he said; and I very generously promised to do so.

'Some weeks afterwards I came across a very fine lot of Havanas in a house I visited rather late at night, and I secured them. The chemist got a box of them.

'"There Mr So-and-so," I said. "I have stolen you these. I hope you will like them." Again he laughed loudly, and he no more believed me than before. Still, I had only told him what was perfectly true.'

Holmes's use of Watson to accompany him on certain burglaries was more in line with the traditional pattern of break-ins carried out at the time. Burglars often worked in pairs, one ransacking the house, the other keeping watch for signals from the 'crow', or look-out, posted outside. As receivers were prepared to fence all kinds of goods stolen from upper class homes, a typical haul could easily include carpets, small items of furniture and paintings, so transport had to be arranged. When the coast

Holmes disguised as a simple-minded clergyman.

The Victorian reading public devoured the lurid accounts of violent robberies and heinous crimes published in the popular magazines.

was clear a horse-drawn cart, or a Hansom cab with false licence plates, would discreetly pull up to take the goods away at a steady trot.

The rise of the affluent middle class in the middle of the century increased the pickings for professional burglars. The jails were full of petty thieves, but the lords of the underworld lived lavishly, many with servants of their own, in houses decorated more luxuriously than those of their victims.

At the other end of the criminal scale, London teemed with pickpockets, footpads, prostitutes and confidence tricksters. They lived in cheap lodging houses, foul rooms overcrowded and without sanitation, and preyed on anyone, from their own neighbours to the toffs strolling the busy streets of the West End. Many were familiar faces to police officers who patrolled these unsavoury beats, and in some districts there was a strong sense of community among criminals.

One stratum of the teeming Victorian sub-culture, however, was a closed door, seldom understood by police and shunned by criminal gangs. Drug trafficking went on relatively unhampered in the warren of dockside lanes. Opium dens flourished in the maze of alleys and wharves flanking the eastern reaches of the Thames. They were frequented mainly by seamen and the Oriental community, but occasionally – as Doyle records in *The Man with the Twisted Lip*, Europeans could be found indulging in a surreptitious pipe or two. It was an aspect of underworld London that Victorian readers found fascinating.

Raids on convoys of ox carts carrying opium on the traditional trails through India were not uncommon, and there were many travellers' tales of its use. But the mysterious rituals of narcotics in the heart of London was intriguing, sensational stuff.

Opium in tincture form was medically recognized as a relief for toothache and other ailments. One or two otherwise respectable people had taken a leaf from Thomas de Quincey's book, *Confessions of an English Opium Eater*, and found the soporific drug too hard to resist.

Among them was Isa Whitney in *The Man with the Twisted Lip*, who soaked his tobacco with laudanum to try to produce the same effects. He became addicted – 'an object of mingled horror and pity to his friends and relatives', Watson tells us. 'I can see him now, with yellow, pasty face, drooping eyelids and pin-point pupils, all huddled in a chair, the wreck and ruin of a noble man.'

This was June, 1889, and Isa's troubled wife Kate begged Watson to collect him from The Bar of Gold, an opium den in Upper Swandam Lane, 'a vile alley lurking behind the high wharves which line the north side of the river to the east of London Bridge'. The good doctor descended a steep flight of steps between a slop shop and a gin shop to encounter a scene familiar to readers of the yellowback novels of which Watson himself was so fond. The long, low basement room, thick with brown opium smoke, was divided on either side into wooden bunks where bodies reclined in 'strange fantastic poses'.

Doyle's quest for realism occasionally led him onto unfamiliar ground. First-hand research in the lower regions of dockland would have been highly inappropriate for a respectable suburban family man from South Norwood, and dangerous into the bargain. Yet, for a page or so, he gives us colourful and graphic details of the interior, customs and habits of The Bar of Gold. Six months before *The Man with the Twisted Lip* appeared in *Strand*, the magazine ran a vivid confession, anonymously written, of a

*Strand* visits The Bar of Gold.

visit to an opium den on Ratcliffe Highway; the same establishment that Charles Dickens had visited to partake of a puff of the tantalizing drug (he was thoroughly sick). The reporter, waiting for his pipe to be prepared, was 'not a little surprised by the entrance of a young, and by no means ill-looking Englishwoman, to whom I gave a civil "good evening".'

Any resemblance to a friendly Victorian wine bar ends, however, when he describes the predictably sordid surroundings: 'It was dirty and dark, being lit only by a smoking lamp on the mantel-shelf, and was not much larger than a full-sized cupboard. The walls, which were of a dingy yellow – not unlike the whites of the smokers' eyes – were quite bare with the exception of the one facing the door, on which, incongruously enough, was plastered a coarsely-coloured and hideous print of the crucifixion. The furniture consisted of three raised mattresses, with small tables, on which were placed pipes, lamps and opium.'

In the fictional Bar of Gold, Watson found Holmes lurking in disguise as an old man with 'an opium pipe dangling between his knees'. The intrepid Victorian writer, 'living the news', made his unexpected discovery when he came to leave. After a dream of 'sailing as on a cloud amid regions of blue and buoyant ether', he woke to find his boots, hat and umbrella stolen. To add to the dubious romance of his Eastern evening, he had a blinding headache, and a taste in his mouth like 'a cross between onions and bad tobacco'.

Lurid though such accounts were, nothing quite grasped the imagination of the Victorian reading public like scandal, murder and crimes with a distinct sense of daring. Middle class readers of popular magazines became intoxicated by anything which smacked of adventure. This was, after all, the age in which many families had sons in India, Afghanistan and the Far East, quelling troublesome natives, and occasionally taking a bullet for their pains.

Those left at home to commute to uneventful office jobs became armchair adventurers, with their heads buried firmly in *Strand*. Reporters fed their appetite by assuming the role of a gentleman burglar for the evening, riding police launches to drag the Thames for bodies, or giving

detailed accounts of cool-headed jewel robberies. As a popular writer with a finger firmly on the pulse of his market, Conan Doyle reflected the feeling of the times. 'I've had to do with fifty murders in my career', Holmes said, in addition to 'five hundred cases of capital importance'.

There were jewel robberies in *The Beryl Coronet*; *The Sign of Four*, when the £500,000 Agra Treasure was stolen; *The Blue Carbuncle*, a gem valued at more than £20,000 was taken from the Countess of Morcar;

Inside, the opium den was not much larger than a full-sized cupboard.

and the black pearl of the Borgias, mysteriously missing in *The Six Napoleons*. The history of famous stones is steeped in blood and intrigue, making them perfect material for crime fiction. Holmes holds up the Blue Carbuncle to the light and muses; 'Just see how it glints and sparkles. Of course it is a nucleus and focus of crime. Every good stone is. They are the devil's pet baits. In the larger and older jewels every facet may stand for a bloody deed. This stone is not yet twenty years old . . . In spite of its youth, it has already a sinister history. There have been two murders, a vitriol-throwing, a suicide and several robberies brought about for the sake of this forty-grain weight of crystallised charcoal.'

The Regent Diamond had a similar chequered history from the moment it was found by a slave worker in India's Parteal Mines in 1701. He is said to have cut a deep hole in the calf of his leg, concealed the stone in it beneath a bandage, and allowed the wound to heal over. He escaped and begged a passage on a ship leaving Madras, but the English captain took the gem and threw his passenger overboard. It was eventually acquired by Pitt, the Governor of Madras, who arranged to have it cut in London. The stone was sold to the French Regent, leaving him with a clear profit of £100,000. By the time Doyle was embarking on his first writing efforts, the diamond – and its history – were in the news again as a French parliamentary committee discussed putting it up for sale.

The Orloff Diamond, part of the Russian crown jewels, was originally stolen by a French soldier who prised it from the eye of a Hindu statue. Its sister stone, the Moon of the Mountains, was obtained by a dealer who poisoned an Afghan soldier and dumped his body in the Tigris. The Hope Diamond and the Koh-i-noor, which had a history of torture and murder before the East India Company presented it to Queen Victoria, were also topics of popular myth and gossip.

By Victorian times jewel robberies were firmly established as sensational, headline-catching crimes, and the wealthy made strenuous efforts to protect their collections. The Duke of Brunswick kept his £600,000 diamonds in an iron safe in a room which could only be reached by crossing his study and bedroom. The safe room was criss-crossed with electric wires connected to a system of bells which, in turn, were linked to wall-mounted revolvers angled to fire a hail of bullets in every direction. Two policemen were assigned to almost constant patrol duty to satisfy his fixation that half the criminal underworld had marked him as a target. The old man, 'a worn-out voluptuary and faded beau', was not imagining things. His Paris fortress had attracted the attention of professional cracksmen from all over Europe. Much to the mixed feelings of newspaper readers, it took an English thief to successfully plunder it.

The Duke's personal valet, a Tynesider named Shaw, forged references to get himself the job and settled down to a leisurely undercover surveillance of the security system. He was, in fact, a strategically-placed front-man for a highly expert gang who had interviewed him for the role and made the arrangements. Shaw quickly discovered that his first problem was that the weapons ringing the safe were on hair-triggers, and extremely sensitive to any movement. His opportunity came when the Duke sent for a jeweller to re-set some of his stones, and opened the safe door ready for the man's arrival. The jeweller was delayed and Shaw quickly took his chance, filling a suitcase with gems and making his escape. He was arrested in a sweep of waterfront

The theft of the Orloff Diamond.

hotels in Boulogne and sent down for twenty years.

Two interesting techniques emerge from the crime, which formed the basis for countless successful jewel robberies until the end of the century. The more popular of these was to use the constantly changing tide of domestic servants to report on the layout of a house, planting them in a likely mansion with fake references. Many servants, who were poorly paid to begin with, were left on a subsistence wage when their wealthy employers moved off to country residences for the summer, leaving them in charge of the empty house. The temptation to cut and run, with a substantial share of the burglary proceeds, was resisted only by the most honest, or life-long, retainers. Some householders checked references by calling personally on the servant's previous employer, but this proved so time-consuming, and the forgery racket was so widespread and sophisticated, that it did little to alleviate the problem.

As to the second technique, the most successful jewel raids were the product of careful long-term planning, by a team in which each man had his own special function. The most elaborately planned raid of the era was undoubtedly the great Cornhill

Jewel Robbery, for which seven men and three women eventually stood in the dock. The target – John Walker's two-roomed jewellers at 68 Cornhill – was considered impenetrable. Iron sheets were embedded in the cavity walls, iron doors had observation shutters, and the white-painted safe could be seen by patrolling officers through a system of mirrors. The area was heavily protected by police after hours, who checked local shops at approximately ten-minute intervals. The Walker's had two floors of offices above it, and the whole building was empty at night, preventing the possibility of a 'bent' member of staff remaining on the premises. The business of locking up each night – which included

making sure the upstairs offices were locked and empty – took a laborious three-quarters of an hour. When the final key was turned three gas jets were left burning in each room to give patrolling constables a better view.

The gang watched the premises for seven weeks, as well as Mr Walker's family, so that any member of it could be instantly recognized by a look-out who was posted on the roof. The weak spot in security – quickly spotted by the gang – was that Sir Charles Crossley, who had the first floor office above an adjoining tailor's shop, usually left before Mr Walker locked up. To test the feasibility of the plan they watched for him to leave, ran up a common staircase at the side, and broke into his office, on several

Seven men and thre women were eventually brought to trial for the theft of £6,000 worth of jewels and watches from Walker's, a well-known jewellers in Cornhill, in 1865.

occasions before fixing a date for the robbery.

One Saturday evening before the shop closed they picked the lock of the upstairs office and waited for two hours until the building was empty. Breaking directly through the floor into the jewellers would have attracted attention with clouds of dust and plaster. Instead they cut a hole at one end of the office and dropped into the ground floor tailor's shop on a rope-ladder suspended from a pair of fire tongs. An attempt to break through the wall into the jewellers failed when they encountered iron screening behind the brickwork. Undeterred, they moved into the tailors long basement cutting-room, and cut through the ceiling to within a few yards of Walker's safe above.

The business of cracking the safe had to be done in stages between police patrols. One gang member received signals of their arrival by tugs on a length of string from the look-out on the roof, and relayed the message to his colleagues. Using steel wedges and crowbars it took just thirty minutes to open the heavy iron safe and remove £6,000 worth of jewels and watches.

'I tested the safe with a little wedge to see if it was any use trying it seriously', one of the gang said in a police statement. 'It "held" the wedge. If it had resisted the wedge would fly off. I had to kneel down so as not to be seen by the police who were round every nine minutes, so we often had to stop our work. At last we felt the safe give, which we were rather surprised at, as we expected and were prepared for a more difficult safe to deal with. We then knew we would get the safe open.'

A furious Mr Walker later sued the safe's manufacturers who had certified that it could take at least eleven and a half hours to open. Even the most formidable models presented few problems to experienced cracksmen. In 1877 an official at Wormwood Scrubs prison – still under construction at the time – accidentally locked the governor's high-security safe and jammed the mechanism. A warder was despatched to the carpenter's shop to fetch a housebreaker serving fifteen years. 'When I assured him I was in earnest', the official reported, 'he attacked the safe with one of his tools. In less than three minutes the door swung open; the lock had been quite conquered. It was a first-class safe, too.'

The iron chest of the fabulous Agra Treasure in *The Sign of Four* was 'two thirds of an inch thick all round ... massive, well-made and solid, like a chest constructed to carry things of great price.' Yet when the key was lost Watson effortlessly snapped the hasp by levering it with Mrs Forrester's poker. It was, of course, empty and most of the gems had been scattered in the Thames by Jonathan Small. An interesting postscript to the Cornhill Jewel Robbery could not have escaped Conan Doyle's eye, along with thousands of readers who avidly followed the case. When the gang were rounded up on underworld tip-offs, a Thames river police inspector noticed something glittering at water level below Blackfriars Bridge. He pulled his launch alongside to find two gold watches – thrown in at high tide – which had nestled on a horizontal beam slung across some temporary pilings.

The next day a diver was sent down and recovered five more. 'The river was guarded day and night', according to newspaper reports, 'to prevent an unauthorised hunt for watches. By 1st March (four days later) eight gold watches were yielded up by Father Thames, and by 3rd March, eleven. Only one was found after that, making twelve in all.' Incredibly, seven watches

The Cornhill Jewel Robbery: **1** Sir C. Crossley's office, showing the hole cut in the floor
**2** The tailor's shop with the hole cut in the ceiling **3** Walker's shop with the safe and hole in the floor
**4** The tailor's cutting room, showing the hole in the ceiling.
Reproduced from *Mysteries of Police and Crime* (Vol 3) by Major Arthur Griffiths.

with crystal cases were still working after being hurled sixty feet from the bridge – a fitting tribute to Victorian craftsmanship.

The Agra Treasure had resulted in two murders, the unfortunate result of desperate measures thieves have always taken to obtain precious stones. In one of the most violent robberies of the era an eighty-year-old man who lived alone in a lodge house in Muswell Hill was battered to death with a jemmy in 1896. The gang disconnected the trip wire of an 'alarum gun' in the garden, which would have certainly killed them, and broke into the house to crack open a safe containing gold. In 1886 a similarly violent robbery had occurred when two men called on Julius Tabak, a Euston Road diamond dealer, ostensibly to buy gems. One of them coshed him with a life-preserver before they fled with £1,400 worth of diamonds.

Violence and determination to escape the law were common in the tiny upstairs workshops used by coiners who worked, often as whole families, minting passable 'silver' counterfeit coins. Police and Bank of England investigators always approached suspected dens stealthily as the law demanded evidence of fake coins before a case could be brought. Some coiners held off raiding officers by hurling molten metal or bottles of acid at them while the evidence was hurriedly thrown into the melting pot.

In *Shoscombe Old Place*, Holmes tells of a coiner he ran to ground 'by the zinc and copper filings in the seam of his cuff'. The extent of coining is illustrated by the frequency with which it occurs in the adventures. John Clay in *The Red-Headed League* is described by Holmes as the 'murderer, thief, smasher and forger' – a smasher in criminal cant was a man who passed counterfeit coins. John McMurdo, the fearless Pinkerton man in *The Valley of Fear* revealed that he 'shoved the queer' (passed counterfeit coins) to establish his false identity. In *The Three Garridebs* we come across Prescott, the banknote forger's, den. 'The greatest counterfeiter London ever saw . . . No living man could tell a Prescott from a Bank of England.'

The greatest detail lies in *The Engineer's Thumb*, where Victor Hatherley, a hydraulic engineer, is engaged to repair the coiners' press. They tell him it was used for compressing Fuller's earth. When he is caught examining tell-tale metal filings they lock him in the press room and switch on the machinery to crush him to death.

Two points in the description of the room show that Doyle, as usual, had researched his subjects thoroughly. The room was on the top floor – 'we went upstairs . . . it was a labyrinth of an old house with corridors, passages, narrow winding staircases and little low doors . . .' Though coining was no longer a capital offence after 1832, prison sentences were stiff, and anyone setting up a coin press took elaborate precautions. Melting and stamping rooms were invariably on the top floor, partly to allow hot-metal fumes to escape undetected, but also because of attic windows, which provided good light for detailed finishing work without being overlooked.

The secret panel through which Hatherley avoids being crushed by the press was a standard escape measure. ('I saw a thin line of yellow light between two of the boards which broadened and broadened as a panel was pushed backwards.')

Coiners not only provided themselves with such escape routes, but constructed elaborate booby traps to retain pursuing police. Spiked railings were hinged to spring down, cutting off staircases, and, in one case in Westminster, a deep pit was designed to open at the foot of a flight of stairs. During the chase a posse of police narrowly avoided plunging into it. There were no lengths, it appeared, to which they would not go. In *The Engineer's Thumb*, by the time Watson and Holmes tracked down the house from which Hatherley escaped, the coiners had fled, burning down the building behind them.

One of them had chopped off the engineer's thumb with a butchers's cleaver in an attempt to silence him. Policemen in the non-fictional world faced equally gruelling opposition. A sergeant breaking into an upstairs den in Shoreditch found himself set upon by the coiner, together with the man's wife, teenage daughter and the family bulldog which, according to one account, refused to release its grip on the officer's trousers for half an hour.

Advances in electroplating made coining much easier, and counterfeiters found simple methods of acquiring the latest knowledge without attracting attention. One Fulham operator was found to have a book of press cuttings – replies to seemingly innocent queries he had sent to the advice pages of popular magazines. A *Strand* article about his methods said: 'He would write to periodicals asking such simple conundrums as, "Will you kindly tell me the simplest

Victor Hatherley barely escapes being crushed to death in a coiners' press room in *The Engineer's Thumb*.

way to make a battery?" or "Would you kindly say in an early issue the simplest way to make solder for silver?" He often got replies, which we refrain from publishing, seeing that it gives a very efficacious recipe for the first step towards "making money".'

As a boy Charles Dickens was an avid reader of penny dreadfuls, which had the effect of 'frightening the wits out of my head, for the small charge of a penny weekly; which considering that there was an illustration to every number, in which there was always a pool of blood and at least one body, was cheap'. Victorian pulp fiction and melodrama thrived on murder plots featuring cringing heroines, dastardly villains with waxed moustaches and earnest young heroes who saved the day (but only after a suitable number of corpses littered the pages, or the stage). Real murders, there was no doubt, sold newspapers, and the presses ran hot into the night to satisfy the demand for every last detail decency would allow.

All crime fiction, poor or inspired, inevitably mirrored the celebrated crimes of the day. Often the parallels were unconscious, but inescapable – murder for Victorians was everywhere, washing across the front pages of newspapers, murmured in low conversation in gentlemen's clubs and shouted from street-corner billboards. Deaths from cholera, typhoid and other diseases caused by insanitary conditions were still rife; infant mortality was high and deaths in childbirth one of the burdens of womanhood. Death in its natural form was a fact of life Victorians came to terms with by smothering it with flowers, sentimentality and elaborate tombstones. Sudden death by the bullet, the knife or the garotte opened a floodgate of gossip and emotion. Formal life, with its emphasis on moral values and social niceties, had no way of absorbing its enormity. Murder stood outside everything the straitlaced era represented, and exercised a morbid magnetism. Even Holmes, perhaps the most unshockable Victorian of them all, was not beyond its fascinations: '. . . the most winning woman I ever knew was hanged for poisoning three little children for their insurance money', he told Watson in *The Sign of Four*.

Holmes refers to the *Newgate Calendar*, first published in 1773, which catalogued the crimes of the worst offenders in Newgate Prison, and was periodically updated. The volumes, widely read in the nineteenth century, bristle with kidnap, treason, coining and murder of every description. His own adventures, too, had a liberal seasoning of killings which readers at the turn of the century found most palatable. There was murder for inheritance in *The Speckled Band*, *The Devil's Foot* and *The Hound of the Baskervilles*; blackmail which led to murder (always a popular theme) in *Black Peter*, *Boscombe Valley* and *The Five Orange Pips*; death arising from jealousy or passion in *The Crooked Man*, *The Cardboard Box*, *Thor Bridge*, *The Retired Colourman*, *The Veiled Lodger* and *A Study in Scarlet*; revenge killings in *The Musgrave Ritual*, *The Resident Patient*, *Charles Augustus Milverton*, *Wisteria Lodge* and *The Valley of Fear*. There was murder to cover guilt in *The Empty House*; for gain in *The Reigate Squires*, *The Greek Interpreter*, *The Bruce-Partington Plans* and *The Sign of Four*; even murder by accident in *The Golden Pince Nez*.

Victorian interest in detection made suicides arranged to look like murder particularly interesting. In *Thor Bridge* Holmes reveals how a 'vindictive woman attempted to disguise her own crime and to fasten a charge of murder upon an innocent victim'. He reconstructed the suicide, which had taken place on a bridge, by tying one

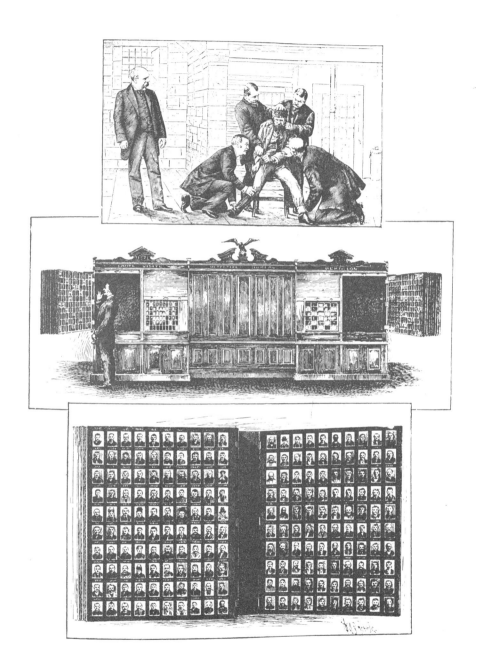

Burglary and violent crimes were on the increase in the Victorian era. To help in the identification of suspects some forces had a Rogues Gallery – though not all prisoners enjoyed having their picture taken.

Murder in *Boscombe Valley*.

end of a length of string to a revolver and attaching a heavy stone to the other. 'He raised the pistol to his head and then let go his grip. In an instant it had been whisked away by the weight of the stone, had struck with a sharp crack against the parapet and had vanished over the side into the water.'

A celebrated Victorian case was that of Risk Allah Bey, 'a doctor of gentlemanly demeanor' who lived in England, but was accused of murdering a youth in an Antwerp hotel. The young man was found shot in his bed by Risk Allah, who claimed that he found the door locked from the inside and a strong smell of gunpowder coming from the keyhole. When police broke down the door they found that it had been barricaded with furniture and the room was full of gunsmoke. It had all the hallmarks of a suicide, but the doctor was arrested because of the strange position of the body. The young man was lying with his arms by his sides, and one hand was under the bedclothes – a position, the police argued, which was incompatible with suicide.

At the trial a similar case was quoted in which a man, even in death, still had the strength to place his arms at the side of his body. It was eventually believed that the victim in the Risk Allah case had used the long ramrod of his gun to press the trigger, so that his arms would drop to his side after the fatal act. Risk Allah was freed, and successfully sued a magazine which had published its own imaginative theory that he was a murderer.

A similar case which attracted the attention of Victorian readers occurred in Savoy, France, in 1885, when an old man was found dead in is bed from a bullet wound to the temple. His eyes were closed, his hands lay by his sides – one of them clutching a revolver – and the bedclothes were pulled up to his chin. For seven years the death was officially accepted as suicide, until there was pressure to re-open the case as a murder investigation, and new medical evidence

was heard. It was generally thought that, in suicides, the corpse retained a firm grip on the weapon. Among the cases cited was that of Captain Nolan, hit by a shell in the heart in the Charge of the Light Brigade, whose sword arm remained above his head and knees stayed gripped to his saddle. A Southern soldier in the American Civil War was also mentioned who was shot as he mounted his horse, and remained with one foot in the stirrup and one on the ground.

Dr Lacassague, a 'medico-legist' from Lyons, was reluctant to accept this. He carried out experiments on hospital patients and made numerous inquiries at the Paris morgue before arriving at the conclusion that a murdered man could also be made to hold a revolver without dropping it. He also argued that, in cases of violent death, the eyes almost without exception remained open. The dead man's had obviously been closed by someone. There were also no scorch marks or powder grains on his temple, which indicated that the gun must

A gruesome discovery. Holmes examines the severed ears in *The Cardboard Box.*

have been held some distance away – a near-impossible task in suicide. The man's son was finally charged with murder and convicted.

Six years after Jack and Ripper terrorized London's East End with a gruesome and baffling series of murders, Conan Doyle wrote *The Cardboard Box*. The plot revolved around a cardboard carton containing the ears of killer James Browner's wife and her lover. For Victorians the story had chilling shades of the Ripper's nocturnal escapades. On 25th September 1888, the Central News Agency received a letter from the murderer which read:

Dear Boss,
    I keep on hearing that the police have caught me. But they won't fix me yet ... I am down on certain types of women and I won't stop ripping them until I do get buckled. Grand job, that last job was. I gave the lady no time to squeal. I love my work and want to start again. You will soon hear from me, with my funny little game.
    I saved some of the proper red stuff in a ginger beer bottle after my last job to write this with, but it went thick like glue and I can't use it. Red ink is fit enough. I hope. Hah,ha!
    *Next time I shall clip the ears off and send them to the police just for jolly.*
    Jack the Ripper


A week later two more bodies were found. The first, lying beneath a factory gate, was unmutilated, suggesting that the killer had been disturbed. But a short walk away police came across the butchered remains of forty-year-old Catherine Eddows, whose ears had been hacked off.

Public imagination was also fuelled by criminal secret societies which were active in Victorian times. Inspector Lestrade had a working knowledge of the Mafia, and

mentioned in *The Sign of Four* that Pietro Venucci had connections with them. In *The Valley of Fear*, the second part of the story is called 'The Scowrers', an account of the clandestine and violent workers' organization and the mass arrests carried out after infiltration by a Pinkerton agent.

The adventure of *The Red Circle*, which appeared in the March and April issues of *Strand* in 1911, was curiously topical. Gorgiano, 'a man who had earned the name of "Death" in the South of Italy, for he was red to the elbow in murder' was ritually murdered by a former member of the Red Circle. The organization was 'a Neopolitan society ... allied to the old Carbonari'. Gorgiano, with Holmes, Watson, Gregson of Scotland Yard and Leverton of the Pinkerton Agency all dogging his tracks, was discovered dead in a third-floor room.

'In the middle of the floor of the empty room was huddled the figure of an enormous man, his clean-shaven, swarthy face grotesquely horrible in its contortion, and his head encircled by a ghastly crimson halo of blood, lying in a broad wet circle upon the white woodwork.'

On 5th January of the same year, about the time Doyle wrote the story, a widely reported inquest in to the death of Leon Beron, murdered on Clapham Common, was hearing medical evidence from pathologist Dr Frederick Freyburger. The tiny courtroom was crammed with Fleet Street reporters who stampeded to their newsrooms when the doctor stepped down from the stand. Beron's murder, he suggested, was the result of a ritual slaying by a secret organization.

'Under the right eye', he told the coroner, 'there was an open S-shaped cut through the outer skin only. It was two inches long and ran across the right cheek in a downward direction. Lower down was a superficial cut in a slanting direction to the middle of the upper lip. There was a similar S-shaped cut on the left side of the face.'

The story was front-paged in all the papers the following day, with the *Daily Mail* running a headline 'THE SIGN OF S'. Like the adventures of Sherlock Holmes, it was superbly chilling stuff.

Doyle, however, gave his stories a depth and dimension which went beyond the most powerful newspaper stories of the day, while losing none of their immediacy. Which, perhaps, is why they have outlived even the most sensational murders of the day in the mind of the reading public.

# Detection

HOLMES'S METHOD WAS based on the simplest rules of observation and reasoning, yet to the casual reader it gives the impression of being highly original. 'I see it, I deduce it', summed up the technique which has intrigued and captivated 150 million readers since the stories were first published. From the manner in which Lestrade and his Scotland Yard colleagues were always two paces behind Holmes's lightning leaps of deduction, we can safely asume that the police's own detective code was more pedestrian.

With the merest fragments of evidence Holmes can tell the astonished Lestrade that the murderer '. . . is a tall man, left-handed, limps with the right leg, wears thick-soled shooting boots and a grey cloak, smokes Indian cigars, uses a cigar holder and carries a blunt penknife in his pocket. There are several other indications, but these may be enough to aid us in our search.'

Holmes was aided by a memory blessed with almost total recall, enabling him to sift 'thousands of similar cases' when he had a glimmer of the course of events. Information, no matter how trivial, was stored in the great brain, waiting to be called up when required. 'Data! data! data!' he cried in *The Copper Beeches*, 'I can't make bricks without clay.' Armed with the Method, the slimmest piece of evidence could, he believed, lead to far-reaching and accurate deductions. 'The ideal reasoner', he remarked, 'would, when he has once been shown a single fact in all its bearings, deduce from it not only all the chain of events which led up to it, but also all the results which would follow from it.'

Doyle gives us the impression that the police were prone to making unsound assumptions and wild guesses, which often led to the wrong conclusions. Holmes was wary of impatient theorizing, and knew from experience that all might not be what it seemed. 'As a rule', he believed, 'the more bizarre a thing is the less mysterious it proves to be. It is your commonplace, featureless crimes which are really puzzling, just as a commonplace face is the most difficult to identify.' We are led to believe from the conduct of Scotland Yard at the scene of a crime that Victorian textbook deduction was a primitive affair. Holmes poked gentle fun at the hapless efforts of Lestrade and Gregson, refusing to venture any opinion himself until he had his precious facts. 'It is a capital mistake to theorise before one has data,' he said. 'Insensibly one begins to twist facts to suit theories, instead of theories to suit facts.'

Having mastered the technique it was, of course, only human to milk it for its maximum effect. Holmes took a quiet delight in astonishing people with the most penetrating remarks, simply to observe the effect his art had on them. 'You see, my dear Watson', he intoned at one of his fireside lectures, 'it is not really difficult to construct

IN THIS NUMBER—"THE RETURN OF SHERLOCK HOLMES"
Beginning a New Series of Detective Stories by A. CONAN DOYLE

# Collier's
## Household Number for October

VOL XXXI NO 26          SEPTEMBER 26 1903          PRICE 10 CENTS

DRAWN BY FREDERIC DORR STEELE

An American magazine, *Collier's*, serialized the adventures of Sherlock Holmes. The October 1903 issue features *The Return of Sherlock Holmes*. The Holmes stories were enthusiastically received by American readers.

The classic profile of Sherlock Holmes graces the front cover of the November 1903 issue of
*Collier's* magazine.

Holmes and Watson in search of hard evidence in *The Musgrave Ritual*.

a series of inferences, each dependent upon its predecessor and each simple in itself. If, after doing so, one simply knocks out all the central inferences and presents one's audience with the starting-point and the conclusion, one may produce a startling, though possibly a meretricious effect.'

In *The Dancing Men* he demonstrated his point by suddenly remarking: 'So, Watson, you do not propose to invest in South African securities?' The good doctor, to Holmes's evident satisfaction, was quite taken aback. Having achieved the effect, the detective explained the missing links in the chain:

'1. You had chalk between your left finger and thumb when you returned from the club last night.

'2. You put chalk there when you play billiards to steady the cue.

'3. You never play billiards except with Thurston.

'4. You told me four weeks ago that Thurston had an option on some South African property which would expire in a month, and which he desired you to share with him.

'5. Your cheque book is locked in my drawer, and you have not asked for the key.

'6. You do not propose to invest your money in this manner.'

Circumstantial evidence, perhaps above everything, may trap the unwary, laying false trails to distract a detective's essential objectivity. Holmes was well aware of the problem. 'Circumstantial evidence is a very tricky thing', he once remarked. 'It may seem to point very straight to one thing, but if you shift your own point of view a little, you may find it points in an equally uncompromising manner to something entirely different ...' Doyle himself was unhappy that irretrievable conclusions could be drawn from circumstantial evidence alone, and wrote articles for *Strand* on the problem.

The disturbing possibility that someone could be wrongly imprisoned as the result of false reasoning was brought sharply home to him as he leafed through the pages of *The Umpire* in 1906. He read the disconcerting story of a young lawyer whose father, an Indian, was vicar of Great Wyrley. Despite the cleric's pleasant manner, and the fact that he was married to an Englishwoman, parishioners in the Staffordshire back-water were still steeped in suspicion and nineteenth-century attitudes to foreigners. When local farmers discovered their horses slashed and maimed by a maniac, the police linked the crime to a series of anonymous letters residents had been receiving. Then, with little more than fantasy to guide them, they connected the letters to George Edalji, the vicar's son. Doyle took a leaf from his own creation, and applied himself to the case with Holmesian determination. After interviewing the family and studying transcripts of the trial, he came to the conclusion that Edalji was completely innocent. Apart from his unblemished record there was not the slightest possibility that he could have committed the crime. Doyle, with his ophthalmic knowledge, proved that the accused was far too short-sighted to

Holmes, in pursuit of a murderer in *The Boscombe Valley*, examines a pair of boots.

have even crossed a field, let alone located an animal in it.

His findings, written in a series of articles for the *Daily Telegraph*, resulted in Edalji being freed after serving three years of a seven-year jail sentence, and reinstated by the Law Society. There now came an ironic twist to the daily flood of mail at Doyle's home. Letters arrived addressed to him, not Holmes, begging him to solve cases. It was difficult to decide which was the more tiresome, but there was little he could do to stem the tide. Answering them all would have made impossible demands on his time, but the correspondence showed no sign of abating. Doyle read them all and discarded them – but two years after the Edalji affair a plea landed on his doormat which undermined his resolve.

He read and re-read the letter with little enthusiasm, but a sense of humanity urged him to make further inquiries. It took the efforts of Doyle, and several others, almost twenty years to secure the release of Oscar Slater, wrongly imprisoned for the murder of an old lady in Glasgow. It was a sordid case with witnesses finally admitting that they had been paid to lie by both police and the Procurator Fiscal. And even when the appeal came down on the side of justice, Doyle found himself at odds with Slater about who should pay the balance of the legal expenses. Holmes would have handled it with more aplomb, but real life always has a myriad of loose ends. It was a messy business which would have incensed the detective as much for its stupidity as it concerned Doyle for its lack of justice.

The police came out of the case very badly, but in the Holmes stories Doyle portrayed them, on balance, as well-meaning, misguided bunglers rather than malicious. But were they really as inept as he made them appear? Let us for a moment go back to Holmes's demonstration – the billiard chalk on Watson's thumb and his decision not to invest in South African securities. The effect of such brilliant deductions was dramatic. The simplicity of the explanation, and its elementary logic made the reader feel that such powers were within his grasp. One of the great appeals of the adventures is the clarity of reasoning, dangled like a carrot until the last possible moment. A moment that offers welcome release after the tensions of the plot.

'People give me great praise for some extraordinary powers. It is all nonsense. I am just in the position of the candid juggler, who tells his audience that there is no mystery at all in his art, when all is explained. My deductions have been, and are, very simple pieces of business . . .'

Holmes enthusiasts would search in vain, however, for these words in any of the adventures. They were spoken by an extraordinary detective solving cases in Edinburgh when Dr Joseph Bell, master of the Method, was a mere medical student. Is it coincidence that twenty-five years later Holmes was echoing his words? 'You know a conjuror gets no credit when once he has explained his trick; and if I show too much of my method of working, you will come to the conclusion that I am a very ordinary individual after all.'

James McLevy was a legend in the granite city in the same way that Bell was to become one years later. Three years after Bell received his medical degree at the age of twenty-one, McLevy was publishing two volumes of his reminiscences of thirty years of detective work. Later, when Bell the senior consultant worked closely with Edinburgh police on criminal cases, stories of the exceptional Mr McLevy were enjoying a renaissance. 'He was not only the best and most successful detective in Scotland, but perhaps outstripped all his rivals in England too', wrote the late George Scott-Moncrieff in an introduction to a collection of McLevy's best cases. Scott-Moncrieff, one of the best-loved figures on the Edinburgh literary scene, makes the point that the Irishman, who had a firm grasp of the Method when Bell was still at school, must also have been familiar to Conan Doyle.

In 1878, fiction writer William Crawford Honeyman penned a series of detective short-story books under the name of James McGovern. The stories were thinly-disguised cases, given a little journalistic 'top-spin', from McLevy's own memoirs. They poured from Edinburgh publishers under such titles as *Brought to Bay, Hunted Down* or *Tracked and Traced*, which alone sold 25,000 copies before foreign rights were sold to France and Germany. Unfortunately no-one hunted down or brought to bay the opportunist Mr Honeyman for plundering the experiences of a most singular police officer. They were published when Doyle was a medical student at Edinburgh, saving his lunch money to spend on books. Browsing the teeming shops of Prince's Street he could not have failed to notice them.

'McLevy, like Professor Bell, was exceptionally quick at observing and drawing conclusions from scanty evidence', Scott-Moncrieff wrote. 'As he himself says, he developed his susceptibilities in such a way that what might have seemed mere luck or coincidence became part of his professional know-how.'

McLevy's own book, *The Sliding Scale of Life*, reveals glimpses of his technique. 'There is a great deal more in faces than is generally supposed', he wrote. 'All men and women pretend, more or less to the subject, but really their study is generally limited to the inquiry whether one is pleased or dis-pleased with you when in a talk. How few ever aspire to read people as they run, to guess what they are bent upon, and how things are going with them; and yet what a field is open to the student of human nature here! ... I can, for instance, always tell an unlucky thief from a lucky one – one with speculation in his eye from one with empty pockets – one who suspects being scented from one who is on the scent.'

Or, as Holmes more succinctly put it: 'My eyes have been trained to examine faces and not their trimmings. It is the first quality of a criminal investigator that he should see through a disguise.'

McLevy in action is amply demonstrated in the Case of the Orange Blossom, when he dramatically arrested a bride at her wedding on theft charges. In 1842 sixteen homes had been broken into in just six weeks by someone using skeleton keys. McLevy's superior was worried that the Edinburgh force was losing face: 'Aberdeen will mock, and Berwick hold up a finger at us. What's to be done?'

At this point, in true Holmesian fashion, McLevy informs his boss that there is only one thief, she is a woman and on the point of getting married. To prove his point to the astonished Lieutenant, he pulls from his pocket a tiny scrap of fabric 'not larger than two crown pieces'. It had been found by a householder at the scene of the last break-in and McLevy, inquiring at a local broker's, had matched it to a dress recently bought there. The range of items stolen from the houses was strange – a pair of boots here, a garment there, gloves, jewelry and a sprig of orange blossom.

McLevy correctly deduced that the thief was a hawker he had seen in the neighbour-hood. 'Her face was that of a gypsy, with the demureness of the race mixed with a simplicity, which they seldom exhibit. Her

'No crime, but a very great error has been committed'; Holmes secures the release of an innocent man in *The Man with the Twisted Lip*.

dress, plain almost to Quakerism, had all that dandyism which extreme care and an excellent taste can bestow on very plain things.'

McLevy tracked the girl, Elizabeth Gorman, to her wedding where he stood among the guests. 'I scanned Elizabeth's dress – a fine lavender *glacé* silk, adorned with as many knots as would have bound all the lovers in the room in silken bands; collar and sleeve of lace, of what kind goes beyond my knowledge; grey boots, necklace and armlets; white kid gloves with no doubt many rings under them ... according to my recollection of my list, I saw a perfect heaping up of all manner of things collected from the sixteen opened houses which the pretty bride had so industriously entered.'

Their eyes met as she turned to survey her guests. She recognized McLevy but gave nothing away – 'no additional paleness, no quiver of the lip, no hairbrained glances of fear'.

'And who are you?' she asked calmly. 'You are not invited.'

'No, I have taken the liberty of inviting myself.'

By this time the rough and ready crowd had also recognized him and were murmuring about throwing him out. 'To all this I paid little attention. I was more curious about a movement on the part of Elizabeth, whose right hand was apparently fumbling about her pocket. A pocket in a bride's dress! ay, just so. Elizabeth Gorman was a bride of a peculiar kind; she had a *pocket* even as part of her bridal apparel, and there was more there than a cambric handkerchief.

'"I will help you get out your napkin, Elizabeth," said I. And putting my hand into the sacred deposit, I pulled out two check-keys. With these keys she had opened the whole sixteen houses.

'"And the orange blossom," said I. "I have a fancy for this too," I said as I, very gently I hope, took off the wreath and, in spite of the necessary crumpling of so extreme an emblem of bliss, put it in my pocket.'

Then, addressing the shaken guests, McLevy announced: 'I choose to claim this young woman for my bride', and took her away to be charged.

The denouement had a certain Holmesian melodrama; the technique not quite as polished as when, a quarter of a century later, Doyle began refining it. But McLevy, nevertheless, is unmistakeably a detective in the mould of Bell and Holmes. Like many who toiled for long years among the lower depths of Victorian society, he became, as journalists put it, 'case-hardened'. McLevy thought nothing of going to lengths which would offend our twentieth-century sensibilities to secure a conviction. His efforts, patient reasoning and obvious love of his work helped policing generally through its awkward transition from a job to a vocation.

He was once approached by a scavenger clutching a parcel. The frightened man, who combed Edinburgh's Royal Exchange district, watched while McLevy unwrapped it and found the severed leg of a small child. He had retrieved it from an open sewer at the back of a tenement block. Arriving at the scene, McLevy happened to glance up in time to see the pale face of a girl withdrawing from a window high in the back of

an adjoining inn. Shortly afterwards, he knocked at the door, and she opened it – 'The same countenance, delicate and interesting, the same nervous eye and look of shrinking fear; but now a smart cap upon her head, which was like a mockery of her sadness and melancholy'.

The detective discreetly interviewed the landlord in private. He was adamant that the girl had not been pregnant, but agreed that she did look paler than usual. From studying her face and movements, McLevy was convinced he had his woman. The problem was that, despite his certainty, he had no proof and she could easily deny everything. He decided on his plan and returned to the office, where he wrapped the limb in fresh paper and addressed it to her. Within the hour he was back at the inn, knocking on the door.

'Tell her I have a parcel from the country for her', he said.

'At length I heard someone at the door. She was not pale now; a sickly flush overspread the lily – the lip quivered – the body swerved. She would have fallen had she not called upon a little resolution not to betray herself.

'"What – you have a parcel for me, sir?"

'"Yes, Mary," said I, as I still watched her looks, now changed again to pure pallor.

'"Where is it from?" she said with increased emotion.

'"I do not know," said I, "but here it is," handing it to her.

'The moment her hand touched it, she shrank from the soft feel as one would do from that of a cold snake, or why should I not say the dead body of a child? It fell to her feet, and she stood motionless, unable to move even a muscle of her face.

'"That is not the way to treat a gift," said I . "I insist on your taking it up."

'"Oh God, I cannot!" she cried.

'"Well, I must do it for you," said I taking up the parcel. "Is that the way to treat the presents of your friends; come," laying it upon the table, "come, open it; I wish to see what is in it."'

The girl burst into tears and McLevy secured his confession. His style was tough and relentless, but to his credit he ensured that the sentence, for disposing of her still-born child, was light.

McLevy's method, theatrical and highly original in its day, surfaces repeatedly in his memoirs:

'"Oh McLevy, you're just in time," said the Captain. "Here is Mr Blyth with information that his shop has been broken into last night and a great quantity of silk carried off..."

'"There's no occasion for calling in any of the men," said I. "Neither is there any occasion for troubling the brokers. I know who the robbers are, and will have them up in a couple of hours. Nay, if you wait, I will bring them to you."

'"What," cried the astonished silk mercer, "already! You're surely joking. Have you been up all night?"

'"No, in bed all night, sleeping as sound as a bat in winter."'

The more McLevy relates his tales, the more they assume a familiarity – not in content, but the wry, assured, secretive way in which the forgotten Irishman played to the gallery for his own delight. As Holmes himself said in *The Valley of Fear*: 'The old wheel turns, and the same spoke comes up. It's all been done before, and will be again.'

The Bertillon system of man measurement provided a record of known criminals.

McLevy, operating in the days before forensic science, relied almost totally upon his own deductions. By Holmes's day great strides had been made which took police work to the threshold of techniques employed today. The Baker Street sleuth carried out his own scientific research which appeared to give him an advantage over the slow-witted men from the Yard. He studied handwriting – even typewriting. 'It is a curious thing,' he remarked, 'that a typewriter has really quite as much individuality as a man's handwriting. Unless they are quite new, no two of them are exactly alike. Some letters get more worn than others, and some wear only on one side.'

Holmes wrote a monograph on footprints and believed it to be a neglected art. We find him tracing and examining footprints throughout his adventures. Contrary to his belief, however, the technique was very much alive and in common use in Kirkudbrightshire, Scotland, in 1786, and successfully matched to a pair of hob-nail boots. Soil particles and grains of sand in the culprit's sock fibres also matched conditions at the scene of the crime, and he was convicted.

Before fingerprints were commonly accepted for identifcation, Scotland Yard used the system of anthropmetry, or 'man-measurement', to provide a record of known criminals. The method was developed by Bertillon, a French medical man who gave evidence in the Dreyfus case, on the basis that certain body measurements are individual and unchangeable. The width of the head, the length of the face, and the lower limbs from the knee to the foot were among those taken. Ear and foot dimensions were also measured with calipers and carefully noted as a means of identity, pre-dating Holmes's two monographs on the subject. Only when the

system proved too time-consuming and complicated was it abandoned by the Yard in favour of Francis Galton's fingerprint research.

Holmes, as we know, paid great attention to detail: 'You know my methods are based upon the observation of trifles', he said. The living counterparts of Lestrade and Gregson were also trained in similar observation techniques. By the 1890s the system had become quite refined. 'The best method of procedure is clearly laid down in police manuals', Major Arthur Griffiths wrote in 1896. 'An immediate systematic investigation on the theatre of a crime, the minute examination of premises, the careful search for tracks and traces, for any article left behind, however insignificant, such as the merest fragment of clothing, a scrap of paper, a harmless tool, a hat, half a button ... all these are detailed for the guidance of the detective ... Fingerprints and footmarks have again and again been cleverly worked into undeniable evidence. The impression of the first is personal and peculiar to the individual; by the latter the police have been able to fix beyond question the direction in which criminals have moved, their character and class, and the neighbourhood that owns them.'

We should not be drawn into debating how unique Holmes's methods were; the evidence suggests rather that, when it came to a knowledge of the police, Conan Doyle was not as up-to-date as he might have been. It is more likely that he sacrificed factual detail for the art of story-telling. Holmes has remained a popular hero by towering over those around him.

A year earlier, in 1895, *Strand* carried an article called 'Some Curiosities of Modern Photography' which showed that, even by then, the camera was being extensively used in forensic science. Photo-micrography, as it

'You know my methods are based upon the observation of trifles'; Holmes examines
a small fragment of wood in *The Naval Treaty*.

was called – the technique of taking photographs through a microscope – was developed by two German forensic scientists, Dr Jeserich of Berlin, and the improbably-named Professor Sonnenschein.

Jeserich began to photograph his experiments 'in order to have the whip-hand over other experts who disputed his microscopical observations'. In 1884 he examined a white hair found on the body of a girl murdered in Westphalia, and compared it to a hair from the beard of a man in custody. According to *Strand*: 'The photomicrographs certainly showed that the hairs were in some respects alike. Both had the same pith in the centre; both had the same air-channels, scales and hollow spaces, and a certain fine structure of surface was common to both hairs under examination. For all that, the expert looking at his photos., pronounced the hair found on the body to be that of an animal, solely because the pith extended to nearly the whole width of the shaft.

'But what animal? Further experiments showed that the hair had been plucked from a dog. In every case photo-micrographs were compared and, this fact ascertained, the case grew with amazing swiftness in the expert's hands.

Holmes makes a great forensic discovery in *A Study in Scarlet*.

'From its colour the hair belonged to a yellow dog that was growing old; its circular section and smoothness showed that it belonged to a smooth-haired dog; and from the unclipped point it was deduced that the animal's hair had never been cut. Thus a description of the dog was worded as follows: "An old, yellow, unshaven, smooth-haired and comparatively short-haired dog."

'The man under arrest for this murder was liberated on Dr Jeserich's evidence. Barely a year later suspicion fell upon another person who possessed a dog exactly coinciding with the above description. More scientific investigations followed and, about two months after his arrest, the man confessed that he had murdered the girl.'

In *Shoscombe Old Place*, written in 1927, but set around 1902, Holmes was bending over his low-powered microscope mulling over a similar problem; ' "It is glue, Watson," said he. "Unquestionably it is glue. Have a look at these scattered objects in the field!"

'I stooped to the eyepiece and focussed for my vision.

' "Those hairs are threads from a tweed coat. The irregular grey masses are dust. There are epithelial scales on the left. Those brown blobs in the centre are undoubtedly glue." '

He had been asked to look into this particular case by Merivale of the Yard because 'they have begun to realise the importance of the microscope'. Evidence suggests that several international police forces had already seen its significance. A forensic laboratory had been established at Lyons, and a forensic science training school at Lausanne. However, Britain's first forensic laboratory – set up by Captain Athelstan Popkess, Chief Constable of Nottingham, did not appear until 1932, though

significant strides had been made since the turn of the century.

Holmes appears to have made a great forensic discovery in *A Study in Scarlet*, at the very moment he first meets Watson. The detective's first words to his future companion were: 'I've found it! I've found it! I have found a re-agent which is precipitated by haemoglobin, and by nothing else.' In case Watson had missed the significance of this, Holmes went on to explain: 'Why, man, it is the most practical medico-legal discovery for years. Don't you see that it gives us an infallible test for blood stains.'

Holmes indeed seemed to have made world history. The story was published in 1887, and it was not until 1902 that Bordet, the French biochemist, had his tests on the biochemical analysis of blood accepted as evidence in British courts. Holmes tells us that, compared to his new discovery, 'the old guaicicum test was very clumsy and uncertain. So was the microscopic examination of blood corpuscles. The latter is valueless if the stains are a few hours old . . .' While the evidence of this last remark is doubtful, we can only assume from the fact that Holmes never put his test to practical use in any of the stories, that it proved to be of less consequence than he at first thought.

His only contribution to mechanical invention was a pair of steel, self-locking handcuffs, which we are led to believe he designed himself. 'Why don't you introduce this pattern at Scotland Yard?' he asks Lestrade in *A Study in Scarlet*, taking a pair from the drawer. 'See how beautifully the spring works. They fasten in an instant.'

Inspector Maurice Moser of the Yard provided the answer in a *Strand* article of 1894, confirming that British handcuffs – which had to be fitted and locked – were not well thought of by police. American self-locking cuffs, similar to Holmes's, had in fact been used at the Yard for some time. Perhaps poor Lestrade had been left behind in the rush when they were issued. The article, written after Inspector Moser's retirement from the C. I. D. illustrates the problems that officers faced with old handcuffs:

'English handcuffs are heavy, unwieldy, awkward machines, which at the best of times, and under the most favourable circumstances, are extremely difficult of application. They weigh over a pound, and have to be unlocked with a key in a manner not greatly differing from the operation of winding up the average eight-day clock, and fastened on to the prisoner's wrists, how, the fates and good luck only know.

The lengthy, difficult and particularly disagreeable operation, with a prisoner struggling and fighting, is to a degree almost incredible. The prisoner practically has to be overpowered or to submit before he can be finally and certainly secured.

'Even when handcuffed, we present to a clever and muscular ruffian one of the most formidable weapons of offence he could possibly possess, as he can, and frequently does, inflict the deadliest blows upon his captor. Another great drawback is the fact that these handcuffs do not fit all wrists, and often the officer is nonplussed by having a pair of handcuffs which are too small or too large. When the latter is the case, and the prisoner gets the "bracelets" in his hands

Lestrade puts the darbies on Jim Browner in *The Cardboard Box*.

instead of on his wrists, he is then in possession of a knuckle-duster from which the bravest would not care to receive a blow.

'On the occasion of my arresting one of the Russian rouble note forgers, a ruffian who would not hesitate to stick at anything, I had provided myself with several sized pairs of handcuffs, and it was not until I had obtained the very much needed assistance that I was able to find the suitable "darbies" for his wrists. We managed to force him into a four-wheeler to take him to the police station, when he again renewed his efforts and savagely attacked me, lifting his ironed wrists and bringing them down heavily on my head, completely crushing my bowler hat.

'As the English handcuffs have only been formed for criminals who submitted quietly to necessity, it was considered expedient to find an instrument applicable to all cases. The perfected article comes from America and, being lighter, less clumsy and more easily concealed, finds general favour among the officers of Scotland Yard.'

Inspector Moser, obviously a policeman of the old school, went on to confess that he distrusted all handcuffs, self-locking or not. 'I dislike them', he said 'for in addition to their clumsiness, I know that when *I* have laid my hands upon a man, it will be difficult for him to escape.'

Moser, of course, could speak confidently from the safe distance of retirement. Detectives working on the streets of Victorian England found that arrests were not necessarily as simple as the manual made out. Chief Inspector Jerome Caminada, twenty-five years a Manchester detective, recalled a dawn incident in his memoirs of 1895. 'The woman came down and put on a pair of clogs. I told her she had better come along quietly. But no – she had little inclination to

be taken in that fashion. As I went to get hold of her, she ran to the stairs and a struggle took place in which she threw herself upon the floor ... She succeeded in getting hold of the carved work in front of the dresser, and pulled the dresser across the floor to the door step, where it became wedged. Putting my foot against the edge of the pavement and giving one or two strong pulls, off flew the ornament to which the woman stuck, and down I went on my back with Pretty Betsy on top of me.'

Other reminiscences include being punched on the nose, given a cauliflower ear and being severely bitten ('Fortunately he had no teeth, but he worked away so vigorously with his gums that I could feel the pain for weeks').

Detective Inspector John Sweeney of Scotland Yard was ordered in 1890 to infiltrate the Legitimation League, originally founded in Leeds with the aim of legitimizing illegitimate children. It attracted a bizarre assortment of free-thinkers.

Before Detective Inspector Sweeney's undercover work led to the seizure of several thousand copies of Havelock Ellis's *Psychology of Sex*, he became highly regarded by League members. Little aware of his real identity they invited him to a 'select dinner' at the Holborn Restaurant. As he secretly scribbed notes and tried to memorize faces a photographer arrived and insisted that he should join the official group photograph. With the greatest discomfort he was forced to smile in the company of 'a dozen dangerous anarchists, a "woman who did" (and suffered imprisonment for doing), a miscellaneous bunch of avowed free-lovers, two lady officials of the Rational Dress Society (clad in low-necked "rational" costume), two editors, two poets, a novelist of world-wide reputation, and a baby aged eighteen months.'

I mention Sweeney, not because of the strange company he kept, but for his account of the arrest of an extraordinary character who made Doyle's Prof. Moriarty not such an implausible figure in the Victorian underworld as we might imagine. In all the criminal accounts of the era it is extremely rare to encounter a sinister and elusive master criminal of the calibre of Dr de Villiers. Scotland Yard pursued him for two years, but the doctor – a classic example of a brilliant mind gone wrong – eluded them at every turn.

His real name was George Ferdinand Springmuhl von Weissenfeld, alias de Villiers, Singer, Weller, Wild, Winter, Willing, MacMillan, McCorquodale, von Jarchow, Perrier, Grant, Wilson, Davies 'and a score of other names'. He was born in Germany, where his father was an eminent judge, and brought up in luxury. De Villiers had a formidable intellect, obtaining degrees with the highest honours in science, medicine and literature. His German wife, also from a highly respected family, remained with him up to his dramatic death when he was finally cornered by the Yard. Like Moriarty, who resigned from a university post because of 'dark rumours', de Villiers broke with his father and fled Germany after forging cheques and securities. In 1880 he settled in London, where he soon fell foul of the law and was sentenced to twelve months hard labour for perjury.

Chief Inspector Sweeney takes up the story: 'On his exit from prison he and his wife disappeared, to emerge as Mr and Mrs Wild, who made a fairly good living by various questionable industries. Later he registered the Concentrated Produce Co. Ltd., inventing various names under which he appeared as shareholders, managers and directors, all in one. This company was a fraud like all the rest of his businesses, and

was wound up after it had served its turn providing him with a few thousand pounds to spend. In 1891 he promoted a company called the Brandy Distillers Co. Ltd. By the issue of a glowing prospectus, giving photographs of various vineyards, none of which belonged to the company, he managed to get thousands of pounds subscribed. By the payment of regular dividends, he secured immense annual additions to the subscribed capital, and it is estimated that, from this one company he drew about £60,000.

'As in all his companies, Dr de Villiers was himself the only officer, but names were used consistently throughout to give the impression that there were the usual directors, signatories and officials. His aliases were now innumerable, and to avoid confusing the identity of the various characters he had invented, he kept a register in which he entered every alias he used, together with its own specific signature.

'Intricate banking and book-keeping arrangements were made to increase the difficulty of tracing the disposal of the shareholders' monies; for this purpose he and his wife kept going more than thirty district banking accounts in various names and in various London districts.

'To increase his security against identity, his wife, besides being responsible for many of the banking accounts, lived with him as his sister and was said to be the wife of an American philanthropist of enormous wealth. Even his domestic servants were a puzzle, at one time posing as housemaids, nurses or cooks, at other times prodigiously smart in dress, they sat in the drawing-room and were introduced to visitors as wives and daughters of statesmen, ambassadors and celebrities.'

But thanks to Chief Inspector Sweeney's investigations the net was closing in. De Villiers, he realized, had set up a spurious

Detective Inspector John Sweeney.

company, the University Press, forging the names of signatories. (The publishing house, I hasten to add, has no connection with any modern company of a similar name.) His publications, including Havelock Ellis's book, were ordered to be destroyed by magistrates. The Yard, armed with his latest identities, also had a good idea of his whereabouts. Officers moved in under the command of Det. Ins. Arrow and Det. Sgt. Badcock.

Chief Inspector Sweeney: 'In January 1902, acting on information, they entered a well-furnished, expensively rented house called Edenfield, situated in the best residential quarter of Cambridge. De Villiers and his wife were posing as Dr. Sinclair Roland and Mrs Ella Roland. Edenfield had been chosen for its security from observation and its general utility as a hiding place. There was an elaborate system of cupboards, and at the back there were secret passages by means of which the occupants could hide or escape.

'On this occasion every precaution had been taken, every exit was blocked, and after Mrs Roland had made vain attempts at bluffing and the doctor had tried the secret means of egress only to find it closed and secured, a systematic search was made throughout the house. At length a secret panel was discovered revealing a passage just large enough to hold one man. At the risk of his life Sgt Badcock entered stealthily into the dark passage, and flung himself upon a man he found there. Dragged into the light de Villiers faced his pursuers, a haggard fugitive at bay. Fortunately in the struggle a loaded revolver had been knocked out of his hands, and all his courage fled when the handcuffs were put on.

'He listened while the warrant was read to him, making no comment, neither denying his identity nor admitting his guilt. A few minutes later he seemed to develop sudden symptoms of a strange excitement. He called for water. One of the servants of the house ran and filled a glass which was standing on the drawing room table. De Villiers swallowed a few drops of water which seemed as if it were choking him. A few gasps followed, and he fell dead. The most extraordinary criminal of modern times survived his arrest by about half an hour.

'The coroner's jury decided that his strange man died from apoplexy, and there is of course nothing more to be said as to the cause of death. It is probably merely a curious unrelated fact the Dr de Villiers, a doctor, chemist and scientist, used to have in his possession a gold seal ring; in the ring was hidden behind the seal a few grains of a poison which de Villiers boasted years ago would kill a man and leave no trace behind.

'On his arrest the ring was on his hand. Was the story of the poison a myth, or had this dark, unscrupulous man already used his poisons, and shall we find some day that murder must be taken out of the list of the few remaining crimes not known to have been committed by this fascinating criminal?'

Has the Yard come face to face at last with the Napoleon of Crime? Holmes, like Sweeney, had a fierce determination to corner his arch adversary. 'The man pervades London, and no one has heard of him. That's what puts him on a pinnacle in the records of crime. I tell you, Watson, in all seriousness, that if I could beat that man, if I could free society of him, I should feel that my own career had reached its summit ...' Messrs Sweeney, Arrow and Badcock – like Holmes – had that brief satisfaction. Then they returned unassumingly to the sordid back-streets of London, policing the pimps, petty thieves, card-sharps and coiners. Such is the difference between fact and fiction.

## London Street Life

HOLMES'S LONDON WAS a city of the senses. Smells of fruit and flowers, horse dung and open sewers mingled with the clatter of carts and carriages, vendors' cries and the persistent swish of ragged street-sweepers' brooms. With every turn of a corner the scene unfolded and changed. Cabbies waved whips from the boxes of their battered hansoms. Fashionable gentlemen strolled in Inverness capes and pipe-stem trousers, creased 'port and starboard' to imitate the Prince of Wales. Crowds loitered round street entertainers, small boys darted among parading crinolines and horses jostled and shied at busy junctions. As darkness fell gas lamps flared yellow in the Strand and orange on Bayswater Road, individually lit by men with long poles.

The pleasures to be found in the languid surroundings of the opium den appealed to a
surprisingly wide clientele.

*Street Acrobats* by William Weekes (1874). Street entertainers brought pockets of welcome relief to the crowded streets of Victorian London.

Towards the end of the century the population was notching four million – a bustling city going about its business. People travelled on foot, by carriage, or buses drawn by two horses – 'twelve inside, fourteen outside' – with tarpaulins tucked over their knees. Anyone who had the means could take a meal at Gatti's and stroll into Leicester Square where Wyld's Great Globe was a popular attraction. It stood in the middle of the square, a huge globe of the world decorated inside with the continents in plaster relief. Winding stairs led up to platforms from which countries could be inspected at close quarters. Nearby was the Royal Panopticon – later pulled down to make way for the Alhambra Theatre. For a shilling visitors could listen to scientific lectures, receive electric shocks or gaze at the illuminated fountain which rose as high as the roof. In Covent Garden it was fashionable to eat at Evans's Rooms and perhaps glimpse Dickens, Forster or Wilkie Collins deep in conversation over Welsh rarebit or devilled kidneys. Glee singers toured the tables while the host, Paddy Green, dispensed snuff to his favourite guests.

Holmes made it his hobby to have an exact knowledge of London. His rambles with Watson along crowded streets and back lanes gave him an unerring sense of direction. In *The Sign of Four*, when the friends are taken by cab under cover of darkness 'to an unknown place on an unknown errand', Holmes reels off the streets. 'Rochester Row ... Now Vincent Square. Now we come out on the Vauxhall

Holmes and Watson survey the drab houses of London from a train window in *The Naval Treaty*.

Bridge Road. We are making for the Surrey side apparently. Yes, I thought so. Now we are on the bridge. You can catch glimpses of the river . . .'

Victorian London was a city to be savoured, but some quarters were better savoured than others. Beyond the elegant frontages of Regent Street, the gentlemen's clubs of Pall Mall and the stately little churches of the Strand, the city tumbled into the open sewer of the Thames in a haze of fumes from soap boiler's, tanner's yards and back-street slaughter houses. At night, Whitechapel teemed with the lights of restaurants serving dishes from all over the world, alongside whelk stalls and bawdy public houses.

'From tavern to tavern
Youth passes along
With a mouth full of brill
And a heart full of song.'

The sound of Miss Hedenstrom's piano spilled into Leman Street from the Scandinavian Seamen's Home (motto: 'Benevolence knows no difference between nationalities'). Whitechapel, flanked by Aldgate, Commercial Road, Spitalfields, Mile End and the notorious Ratcliffe Highway, attracted all classes of society. By the 1890s it was being cleaned up – slums were disappearing to make way for 'model lodging houses'; the old courtyards, where only a few years earlier the Ripper hacked his victims, were slowly changing. A tough line by magistrates had swept away street entertainers, quietened the music halls and cut down the number of tavern brawls. Girls swung Indian clubs in the Ladies' Gymnastic Club and lights glowed late in the People's Palace where nightschool classes were offered in technical subjects. Much of the area, however, still had vast pockets of resistance – crumbling tenements, narrow dirty lanes and overcrowded rookeries. Children, 'pale and always ailing' ran the streets looking for work and mischief, and concerned Victorians were saddened by their lost opportunities.

The Children's Country Holiday Fund was set up to take them out of the city for a few short days each year, but across London there were still thousands who benefitted neither from charity nor education. Holmes was among the enlightened who saw their potential. As he looked from a train window rattling high on the elevated section above Clapham Junction, he surprised Watson by saying he found it cheering to look down on the drab rows of back-to-back houses. 'Look at those big isolated clumps of buildings rising above the slates, like brick islands in a lead-coloured sea.' Holmes was looking at the Board Schools. 'Lighthouses, my boy! Beacons of the future! Capsules with hundreds of bright little seeds in each, out of which will spring the wiser, better England of the future.'

Holmes's liberal optimism came from his work as a detective, which gave him an intimate knowledge of life on the city streets. It was shared by others in the same profession who resented the sharp class divisions of Victorian society. Years earlier in Edinburgh, Detective McLevy, too, had great compassion for 'the bairns', and was an enthusiastic supporter of Dr Guthrie's Ragged Schools.

Jerome Caminada, the Manchester detective, believed that 'wherever the ruling classes neglect their duties towards those over whom they are placed, they must take the consequences'. Take away the rich man's home and money, he suggested, and let him go into the slums for a while to see how the other half lives.

In his investigations Holmes frequently relied upon the resourcefulness of a small army of
street urchins, the Baker Street Irregulars.

'Change his station in the world that he shall see in those young things who climb his knee – not records of his wealth and name – but little wrestlers with him for his daily bread . . . In lieu of the endearments of childhood in its sweetest aspect, heap upon him all its pains and wants . . . If his fatherly affection outlive all this, send him back to parliament, the pulpit and quarter sessions, and when he hears fine talk of the depravity of those who live from hand to mouth, let him speak up as one who knows . . .'

Holmes, of course, relied on the resourcefulness of a small army of street urchins, the Baker Street Irregulars, and treated them like an avuncular sergeant major. '. . . There rushed into the room half a dozen of the dirtiest and most ragged street arabs that I had ever clapped eyes on. "Tention!" cried Holmes in a sharp tone, and the six dirty little scoundrels stood in line like so many disreputable statuettes.' When they filed their reports he handed each of them a shilling – a generous reward for the period.

Elsewhere in London children were working harder for less pay. Young sweepers supplemented their meagre wages by running errands in the streets they were cleaning. In a good area, perhaps where several Members of Parliament were among their regulars, they were lucky to make 2s. 6d. (12.5p) a week. Holmes, who offered a guinea bonus plus expenses for a job well done, must have been regarded as a gift from heaven. The detective, in turn, was as satisfied as they were – 'There's more work to be got out of those little beggars than out of a dozen of the force', he remarked.

There were times, however, when the Baker Street rooms seemed overrun by them. 'In future they can report to you, Wiggins, and you to me', Holmes ordered. 'I cannot have the house invaded in this way.' He handed them a day's pay in advance and set them out to locate the steam launch *Aurora* on the Thames. As they streamed down into the street, the detective lit his pipe and said; 'They can go everywhere, see everything, overhear everyone. I expect to hear before evening that they have spotted her.' The Baker Street division of the detective force was a tremendous asset, saving Holmes valuable time on routine inquiries. In *The Hound of the Baskervilles* he gives Cartwright, a fourteen-year-old messenger, a list of twenty-three Charing Cross hotels to search for a crucial missing copy of *The Times*, a task that would have taken the detective the best part of a day.

Restrictions placed on employers reduced the number of children working in factories, but created greater problems by throwing more onto the streets to fend for themselves. 'Children find an endless variety of ways of earning a living in the streets', said a magazine article on child workers in 1891. 'There are boot-black boys, who form a useful portion of the community; newspaper boys, of whom the better sort are useful little capitalists with an immense fund of intelligence and commercial instinct; "job chaps", who hang about on railway stations on the chance of earning a few pence in carrying bags; flower girls, match girls, crossing sweepers, who can make a fair living if they are industrious; and lastly – although this enumeration by no means exhausts the list – street prodigies, such as pavement painters and musicians.

'More unfortunate is the lot of some of the little girl workers who assist their mothers at home in tailoring, button-holing and dolls-clothes making. The united work of the mother and child yields only a wretched pittance and, carried on as it is in a room where sleeping, eating and living go on, is of all forms of labour the saddest and

Children as street entertainers.

most unhealthy. Meals consist of bread and tea, and the work is prolonged till midnight by the light of one candle, with the consequence that the children are prematurely aged and diseased.'

Other girls – and a few boys – made a lucrative living as child models, as long as they could dodge the vigilant Board School investigators. A cab driver's daughter, aged fourteen, who posed for Kate Greenaway's books, made £1.10s (£1.50p) a week, working for three artists at a time. Artists actually preferred street urchins; professional models from comfortable families tended to assume stereotyped expressions and poses in the hope of furthering

their career. T. B. Kennington, a popular Victorian child-artist, found ragamuffins more natural, and even ready to suggest ideas themselves.

London took many years to lose its Dickensian character. Not all of it was bad – when tough policing had contained violent crime in the East End it was possible to stroll from the Mint and across the end of Leman Street, in Whitechapel, to the docks through a warren of strange and exotic shops crammed between the sailors' boarding houses, pubs and pawnbrokers. Slop shops, hung with oilskins and sou'westers, carried a ship's figurehead as their sign. Others had windows crammed with foreign

One of the most remarkable shops in Victorian London was Jamrach's in the East End.

A selection of the many strange and exotic objects stocked at Jamrach's.

banknotes, clay pipes, china tobacco jars and sixpenny walking sticks.

Deep in this bargain-hunter's paradise lay Jamrach's – the most famous and disorganized of them all – crammed from floor to ceiling with livestock and bizarre and useless items from every corner of the world. Some gathered dust on the shelves for half a century without being sold, others were eagerly snapped up by collectors of exotica. The Prince of Wales, lured by its reputation, 'stayed long and left much surprised by all he had seen'; Frank 'Bring-em-back-alive' Buckland was also a regular caller.

Jamrach's was perhaps lurking in the back of Conan Doyle's mind when he sent Watson out to fetch a good tracking dog in *The Sign of Four*. The shop, in a row of shabby, two-storied Lambeth houses, was owned by Mr Sherman, 'a lanky, lean old man with stooping shoulders, a stringy neck and blue-tinted glasses'.

'"Step in, sir. Keep clear of the badger, for he bites. Ah, naughty, naughty! would you take a nip at the gentleman?" This to a stoat, which thrust its wicked head and red eyes between the bars of its cage. "Don't mind that, sir; it's only a slow-worm. It hain't got no fangs, so I gives it the run o' the room, for it keeps the beetles down ..."'

Mr Jamrach, who originally came from Hamburg, settled in the East End to open his strange emporium in the 1850s. The residents of Ratcliffe Highway, later St George's Street, never quite recovered. A Bengal tiger was once delivered straight from the nearby docks in a wooden cage and left at his front door. Before he had time to attend to it the animal had broken free and was seen trotting around the corner holding a bewildered street urchin by the scruff of his coat. Jamrach, known to have no fear in such matters, jumped on the beast and laid it unconscious with a crowbar. The boy's father sued for damages, but the sum was covered by a travelling showman, who read the headlines and immediately bought the tiger for £300.

The shop contained monkeys, porcupines, black swans, antelopes, a Sumatra civet cat, and a wild llama which spat at customers. Emus stretched their necks between the bars, pelicans and cranes screeched incessantly and a ferocious black panther dedicated itself to permanently battering down its cage. Sulky crocodiles were force-fed by two sturdy assistants – one to prise open the jaws with a jemmy, the other to ram home a ten-pound lump of meat with a long pole.

Five back rooms held greater delights – hundreds of idols, including a jewelled Buddah; strange arms and armour; Javanese pottery; Maori clubs and African spears; Burmese temple bells and gongs made from skulls. Medieval swords stood shoulder to shoulder with giant sea shells; cow-tail coats with Japanese medicine chests. Most of the stock was bought from passing seamen and sold to museums,

eccentrics and private collectors. The shop has long gone, and with it an irreplaceable piece of forgotten Victorian London.

Dockland was London's melting pot, an exciting blend of danger and delight, but crime as always was never far away. Policing the waterfront was an arduous task carried out by the Thames River Police, who patrolled the murky waters in their gleaming wooden and brass steam launches. They could produce a good turn of speed, leaving Watson to remark in *The Sign of Four*, 'never did sport give me such a wild thrill as this mad, flying man-hunt down the Thames'. The pursuit of the sleek *Aurora* in the adventure put the police launch through its paces.

It picked up Holmes and Watson at Westminster Wharf, where an officer removed its green landing light to disguise its identity. 'There was one man at the rudder, one to tend the engines and two burly police inspectors forward.' Watson remarked that the craft was very fast, shooting past a long line of loaded barges as though they were stationary. Holmes smiled with satisfaction: 'We ought to be able to catch anything on the river.' 'Well, hardly that', said the inspector modestly. 'But there are not many launches to beat us.'

They shot beneath the long series of bridges spanning the Thames, but the *Aurora* began to show signs of pulling away from them. 'We flashed past barges, steamers, merchant vessels, in and out, behind this one and round the other ... "Pile it on, men, pile it on!" cried Holmes, looking down into the engine room, while the fierce glow from below beat upon his eager, aquiline face. "Get every pound of steam you can."'

Conan Doyle indeed piled it on to great effect. The River Police were steeped in the romance of fast chases, the excitement

The Wapping headquarters of the Thames River Police.

of cornering dangerous villains, and the grim drama of fishing bodies from the water. The squad had been hunting barge-thieves since its formation as the Preventative Service in 1792. By 1839 they had reduced the amount of property stolen on the river from one million pounds to one hundred, and become part of the Metropolitan Police. *Strand* lost no time after its launch in sending out a reporter on a typical night patrol from Wapping headquarters. The officers were a tough bunch: 'You may pick out any of these thick-set fellows standing about. They have one and all roamed the seas over. Many are old colonials, others middle-aged veterans from the navy and merchant service – every one of them as hard as a rock, capable of rowing for six or eight hours at a stretch without resting an oar.'

Among the debris washed up and taken

A conjurer.

to the police station over the years were revolvers, rifles, house-breaking tools, a counterfeit bank-note press and a silver cup stolen from Eton which had floated down the Thames from Windsor to Waterloo.

The areas surrounding the river, despite housing and education improvements, were among the poorest in London. Street-corner men were part of the daily scene though, as in *The Man with the Twisted Lip* who made a more lucrative living as a beggar than a clerk, some were not as poor as they seemed. With dexterity and a compelling line of patter many made a reasonable living with an ingenious range of wares:

'The copper wire-worker with the aid of pliers rapidly evolves models of bicycles, flower-stands, vases and card-baskets; the glass collar-stud and "inexhaustible fountain-pen" seller; the little old man who pierces holes in kettles to mend with his patent solder; the proprietor of a patent corn-solvent; the conjuring-cards seller; the boot-blacking stall-keeper; the silverer of old brass articles; the herb-vendor of penny packets to mix with tobacco to destroy the ill-effects of nicotine; the purveyor of old monthly parts of various magazines and periodicals; the umbrella-seller; the conjuror; the open-air reciter, these and many others, with every kind of dodge and manoeuvre to extract pence from the pockets of people are the street-corner men of this great metropolis', a *Strand* journalist wrote in 1891.

A small boy was pulled from the crowd and had his teeth forcibly cleaned with wadding to demonstrate patent tooth powder. A man 'with a fierce eye' stood on a box selling inhalors to cure tooth-ache. Unable to find any sufferers in the crowd, he 'would boldly and thunderingly accuse any particular one of the listeners of sciatica, neuralgia or some other complaint' to the blushing distress of his victim. Street orators always drew large crowds: 'You see before you, ladies and gentlemen, a trained actor and accomplished el-o-cu-tionist who has travelled throughout the whole of the countries of Europe, Asia, Africa and America. I have given recitations in the bleak, frost-laden countries of Northern Russia and Siberiar, in the balmy climates of the South, the burning deserts of the East, and the wild backwoods of America. For a small sum I will give you any recitation you ask for, from Homah to Shakespah. I require sixpence only to get my night's lodgings.'

Other kerbstone characters included the sweetstuff man, selling confectionery at a penny a quarter so fast that two boys had to help him, mohair lace sellers, toy makers, shipwrecked sailors telling tales, song-sellers and street butchers.

The world of Sherlock Holmes lay as much in the crowded streets with the common people as in the quiet drawing-rooms of the wealthy. A century on, its colour and richness are still with us whenever we pick up his adventures.

An accomplished elocutionist.

# A Glossary of Victorian Underworld Slang

**Albert** A gold watch chain which could be weighed in for its scrap value.

**All gay!** The coast is clear – often used by look-outs to mean no police were in sight.

**Anabaptist** Early Victorian slang for a pickpocket who was punished with a ducking under a water pump.

**Angler** A thief who stole from open windows with a hook tied to a stick – the method was all but abandoned by the end of the era.

**Arab** Street urchin.

**Argot** Secret back-talk and rhyming slang of Victorian thieves.

**The awful place** Dartmoor Prison.

**Badger** Thames river thief who killed or overpowered victims and threw them in the river after robbing them.

**Banbury** A promiscuous woman.

**Beak-hunting** Stealing hens and chickens.

**Betty** A skeleton key, also known as a picklock.

**Bit faker** Counterfeit coin maker.

**Broadsman** Cardsharp, or anyone who cheated at cards for money.

**Brother of the gusset** Pimp.

**Brown paper men** Gamblers who bet merely for pennies.

**Bug hunting** The practice of beating up and robbing drunks.

**Cab** Brothel.

**Caddee** A thief's assistant in some low capacity.

**Calfskin, to smack** To take an oath on the Bible, especially in court.

**Candyman** An official writ-server.

**Chiv** A knife; to chiv was to slash someone.

**Chokey** Prison or police custody.

**Cockchafer** A prison treadmill. Prolonged use gave uncomfortable friction burns, hence the expression.

**Cracksman** Safe-breaker, or burglar who forces secure boxes.

**Crib-cracker** Burglar.

**Crow** Look-out man at a burglary.

**Dancer** A cat burglar who breaks in through the roof.

**Dip** Or dipper – pickpocket.

**Dispatches** Weighted dice.

**Drag** To rob from carriages or vehicles – a dragsman.

**Drum** Premises suitable for robbing.

**Dry room** A prison, or cell.

**Duffer** A cheat, particularly someone who sells fake jewelry.

**Early worm** A dawn street scavenger.

**Ebony optic** A black eye.

**Ellenborough's teeth** Spiked railings around King's Bench Prison.

**Esclop** A policeman.

**Eye** A place used by a fence to hide stolen goods.

**Factory, the** Old Scotland Yard.

**Family** Fellow criminals.

**Fine wirer** Skilled pickpocket.

**Fitter** A locksmith who made burglars' tools.

**Flash notes** Paper crudely fashioned to look like banknotes.

**Flatty ken** Lodging house favoured by thieves.

**Flying cove** Someone who sells false information for the recovery of stolen goods.

**Flying the blue pigeon** Stealing lead from roofs.

**Gagger** A confidence trickster who used hard-luck stories.

**Game, on the game** Thieving.

**Gammon the twelve, to** Successfully deceiving a jury.

**Gargler** Cockney slang for the throat – to grab someone by the gargler.

**Garnish, to** To put handcuffs on someone. Out of use by the turn of the century.

**Gift** Stolen property bought cheaply.

**Goddess Diana** Rhyming slang for sixpence (a tanner).

**Green bag** Early Victorian for a lawyer.

**Guy, to do a** To give a false name to the police.

**Hang up, a** A condemned prisoner.

**Hay band** A cheap cigar.

**Hempen fever, to die of** To be hanged.

**Hold out** A pocket or device for concealing winning cards. Used by cardsharps.

**Hustling** Robbing in pairs – one held the victim, while the other took his property.

**Irish man-of-war** Thames barge.

**Jack** Detective.

**Jemmy** Crowbar used for housebreaking.

**Joe Poke** A magistrate (from J.P.).

**Johnny Darbies** Handcuffs.

**Jug** Prison.

**Kate** A skeleton key.

**Ken** A house.

**Kick the clouds, to** To be hanged.

**Kidling** A young thief.

**Kidsman** One who recruited gangs of child thieves.

**Knuck** A pickpocket.

**Lag** Convict, especially one sentenced to transportation.

**Lavender, in** In hiding from the law.

**Leap at a daisy** To be hanged.

**Leaving shop** An unlicenced pawnbroker's.

**Let daylight into someone** To stab or shoot them.

**Lift** A shoplifter.

**Lob sneak** Someone who snatched money from shop tills.

**Lurker** A beggar who traded on hard-luck stories.

**Macer** A cheat.

**Magsman** A cheat or trickster who operated in the street.

**Maltooler** Pickpocket who operated on buses.

**Miltonian** A policeman.

**Mud lark** A Thameside scavenger.

**Mutcher** Thief who robbed drunks.

**Napkin snatching** Stealing silk handkerchiefs.

**Neddy** A cosh.

**Newgate knockers** Sidewhiskers swept back to the ears.

**Nibbed** Arrested.

**Niner** A prisoner serving nine years.

**Noisy dog racket** Stealing brass knockers and letter boxes from doors.

**Off duty** Taking a temporary rest from thieving.

**Old bird** An experienced thief.

**Out of twig** In disguise.

**Over the water** In King's Bench Prison.

**Paddington** Lodging house for vagrants.

**Palmer** Shoplifter.

**Pannyman** Burglar.

**Parlour jumping** Breaking into rooms through windows.

**Peach** A detective.

**Penny swag** Hawker who sells goods in the street for a penny.

**Peter** A safe.

**Preach at tyburn cross** To be hanged.

**Queer diver** Early Victorian for an incompetent pickpocket.

**Racket, stand the** To take the blame in order to protect fellow thieves.

**Rag stabber** A tailor.

**Ramp** A violent robbery.

**Rarzo** Cockney for a man with a red nose.

**Rattle, spring the** Raise the alarm; call the police.

**Reader** Marked card used by cheats.

**Regent** Half a sovereign.

**Ring dropping** To pretend to find a ring and then sell it cheaply.

**Rook** A burglar's jemmy or crowbar.

**Ruffles** Handcuffs.

**Salt box** The condemned cell.

**Screever** One who faked references for servants.

**Scurf** Gang leader.

**Shinscraper** Prison treadmill.

**Smasher** Someone who passed counterfeit money.

**Smug** To steal.

**Snakesman** Supple boy, often chimney-sweep, used to break into houses.

**Snide pitching** Passing counterfeit money.

**Snoozer** Hotel thief.

**Spike** The workhouse.

**Spreading the broads** Playing the three-card trick.

**Stephen** Money.

**Street ganger** Beggar.

**Stretch** A year in jail.

**Super screwing** Stealing watches.

**Tatts** Loaded dice.

**Terrier crop** Convict hair-style.

**Tiddlywinker** A cheat.

**Tie up** A knock out blow (from boxing slang).

**Timber merchant** A street match-seller.

**Toffken** A wealthy household.

**Tooling** Pick-pocketing by experts.

**Tom Sawyer** A lawyer (rhyming slang).

**Tombstone** A pawn ticket.

**Tree moon** Three months in prison.

**Twirls** Skeleton keys.

**Under and over** A swindle (usually found in fairgrounds).

**Up in the stirrups** Wealthy.

**Vamp** A robbery.

**Verge** A gold watch.

**Village butler** A petty thief.

**Virtue rewarded** To be taken away in a prison van (the vehicles had V:R emblazoned on the side).

**Wedges** Marked cards cut narrower at one end.

**Weighing the thumb** Giving short measure by depressing the scales with the thumb.

**Whitechapel brougham** A coster-monger's cart.

**Yack** Early Victorian for a watch.